MW00633180

An Apartment Next to the Angels

Interfaith Imagination ◇ *Discernment* ◇ *Spiritual Legacy*

Melanie-Préjean Sullivan

© 2022 Melanie-Préjean Sullivan

All rights reserved. No portion of this book may be used or reproduced in any manner whatsoever, except for academic or review purposes, with proper citation.

Published by Mystic Peregrine Press; Louisville, Kentucky, U.S.A. www.mysticperegrine.com

Unless otherwise noted, the Scripture quotations contained herein are from the New Revised Standard Version Bible, copyright © 1989 by the Division of Christian Education of the National Council of Churches of Christ in the U.S.A. Used by permission. All rights reserved.

Book and cover design by Rebecca Kueber
Cover art Summer Breeze *by Pavlína Kašparová*

ISBN: 9780578369563 (pbk.)
ISBN: 9780578381596 (ebook)

Mystic Peregrine Press ⚭ Louisville, Kentucky

To the women of the
Margaret Beaufort Institute of Theology
with profound gratitude

Endorsements

This bounty of beautiful stories is Melanie-Préjean Sullivan's spiritual legacy, and a guide to all who seek to discern the connections between self, soul, and world. Read and rejoice!"

— Eboo Patel, Founder President of Interfaith Youth Core and
author of *Acts of Faith: The Story of an American Muslim,
the Struggle for the Soul of a Generation.*

In the tradition of Cajun storytelling, Melanie has woven her tales into explorations of meaning and purpose. She confronts serious issues with humor and care, discerning how we can be open to the Spirit of love and forgiveness. Melanie invites us to ponder our own questions, to write our own stories, to find hope. If our good God is in charge of anything, it's getting good words into the hearts of the people through books of the most ordinary souls.

— Sr. Helen Prejean, CSJ, author of *Dead Man Walking*
and *River of Fire: My Spiritual Journey.*

Melanie-Préjean Sullivan has been touched by the angel of interfaith dialogue, especially the encounter between the Church and the Jewish People. She takes the reader on a journey, exploring some of life's most fundamental questions. Her personal encounters, both ecumenical and interfaith, demonstrate a spirituality that is both profound and at the same time remarkably simple. *An Apartment Next to the Angels* is an engaging, enchanting, and deeply personal reflection. Through the use of narratives, notably Jewish midrash, she tackles deep philosophical questions with ease and the reader comes away both informed and sustained. I commend this book to you.

— Dr. Edward Kessler, Founder President of the Woolf Institute, Cambridge
and author of *An Introduction to Jewish Christian Relations.*

What better way to magnify the critical importance of interfaith and interspiritual work than by storytelling? Melanie-Préjean Sullivan gifts readers and leaders in religious communities and the academy with deep insight gained through years of experience in campus ministry and as an ecumenical and interfaith chaplain. This book is an excellent and outstanding resource for personal reflection and will be useful as a guide for groups. One of the most significant aspects of Sullivan's writing is that you get a clear sense that she isn't just sharing a story, she *embodies* it. Her storytelling invites readers to create innovative and inclusive spaces for dialogue across religious traditions and to discover their own "true self" by cultivating spiritual friendships.

> —The Rev. Dr. Elizabeth L. Hinson-Hasty, Professor of Theology and Religious Studies at Bellarmine University and author of *Dutiful Love: Empowering Individuals and Families Affected by Serious Mental Illne*ss.

Melding personal experience, delight in religious difference, and theological playfulness, this book offers a spirituality that is simultaneously an invitation to discover "joy in the journey" for oneself. There is exciting stimulus on every page.

> —The Rev. Dr. Alan Race, Editor for the journal of the World Congress of Faiths, *Interreligious Insight* and author of *My Journey as a Religious Pluralist: A Christian Theology of Religions Reclaimed.*

A personal testimony reflecting on many years of pastoral experience, this book does discernment rather than talking about it. In its breadth of reference and vivid portrayals of every kind of human situation and reaction it articulates the essence of theological and spiritual reflection, showing it to be accessible to all faith seekers and vital for spiritual health.

> —Sr. Gemma Simmonds CJ, Director of the Religious Life Institute, Margaret Beaufort Institute of Theology, Cambridge.

Melanie is a modern sage who passes on her wisdom by sharing compelling stories from her life, gently encouraging the reader to revisit life's significant moments. By attending to the various dimensions of the spiritual journey (i.e., relationship with God, interfaith understanding, need for discernment, awareness of aha moments, listening twice as much as talking), I was engaged from cover to cover.

> —Dr. Michael Galligan-Stierle, Past president, Association of Catholic Colleges and Universities

Contents

Prologue

For me to be a saint means to be myself. Therefore, the problem of sanctity and salvation is in fact the problem of finding out who I am and of discovering my true self.
—Thomas Merton (*New Seeds*, 31)

Three bookcases held pride of place in the living room of my childhood. On one of the shelves, there was a multivolume collection bound in beautiful colors, shades of blue, green, and purple. The first volume contained a collection of illustrated nursery rhymes; the second, short stories for new readers; while the last volumes contained fairy tales, ancient myths, and condensed versions of the classics. Once I learned to read, I sat for hours with those books.

"Look it up!" my dad would say almost anytime we asked a question. I think we might have initially resented the assignment. Just as easily, he could have answered our question, but without looking up from his own reading, he sent us to a dictionary or an encyclopedia.

Eventually, we realized what he was doing. If we looked up one word, we'd likely stay on the double-paged spread to read the words before and after the one we looked up, and glance at one or more of the tiny black-and-white illustrations of nouns, skimming through and learning a few more words in the process. Similarly, when we went to the encyclopedia, we'd read the other entries near the one for which we'd searched. We always learned more than simple answers to our questions.

When I think back on these experiences, I realize that my own life has been about asking questions, looking for answers, and learning more than I initially thought I would. I majored in history for my first two university degrees in search of the *rest of the story*. I was an archivist and a registrar for a museum. Later, my questions led me to degrees in educational psychology, theology, and ministry, with more library collections at my fingertips.

SPIRITUAL LEGACY AND ETHICAL WILL

Besides consulting reference books or participating in coursework, we need advisors for our most important questions and decisions. As I began to look toward retirement, I met with a financial planner for advice about investments and with a lawyer to review my will. While I think economic plans and financial legacies are important, I also want to leave a spiritual legacy, a document or collection of essays that tells my stories to allow those who follow me to see how I have processed life's ups and downs, life's ultimate questions.

In his book on surviving the Nazis, *Man's Search for Meaning*, Jewish neurologist and psychotherapist Viktor Frankl taught us that our psychological health, in even the most unspeakable situations, is connected to our personal definitions of the meaning of life and our ability to imagine the future. Such personal definitions are our answers to ultimate questions of meaning, purpose, and the future: *Who am I? Why am I here? What am I called to be in this life? How has my being made a difference? Why is there suffering in the world? What will happen when I die?* These kinds of questions are answered over a lifetime. They are not multiple choice or short-answer questions, and they have no formulas to fill in for a quick response.

As I moved through my seventh decade on this Earth and into retirement, I found that these ultimate questions were more important to me than ever. My attempts to answer them in writing these essays form what my Jewish friends call an ethical will (Hebrew: *zava'ah*). My answers are what I have learned in trying to live my most authentic life, using ethical guidelines to make choices. I leave these personal answers in my search for meaning and purpose as a spiritual legacy for those who will follow me, and I invite my readers to do the same.

DISCERNMENT

When I worked as a middle/high school student development counselor and as a university minister, students and colleagues often asked these same kinds of ultimate questions. The most frequent ones were about career choices and vocation, questions which became the topic of my doctoral project on discernment.

The Latin word *discernere* means to separate, to distinguish accurately one object from another. This separation or process of distinguishing choices is critical to mature discernment. My project tested whether there were practical skills we could cultivate to assist us in proper discernment: exploring our essential beliefs or worldviews; reflecting on or journaling with theological questions; writing our spiritual autobiographies; reading about the lives of those we admire; listening to stories of discernment; learning to leave room for doubt; and abandoning people or situations which no longer serve us. My conclusion was that these practical skills could be taught and nurtured. Some of them are explored in this collection of essays, which you are about to read.

PERSPECTIVE AND WORLDVIEW

The ultimate question of personal identity, "Who am I?" has intersectional answers. We are more than merely our job titles, ethnicity, gender, or marital status. We are all of them plus our heritage and religious affiliation, if any. While I identify as Catholic, I often do so with lots of qualifiers to distinguish me from certain groups within that tradition. I find it insufficient to accept simple Catholic answers to help me know my "true self" referred to by Thomas Merton. The most satisfying answers for me have come from my over 50 years of involvement in Jewish-Catholic study and dialogue, and you'll find references to these throughout the book.

I have also discovered that across many religious and nonreligious worldviews, there are more similarities than we might have learned from those who taught us only from their one perspective. Stories of spiritual encounters within Abrahamic, Eastern, blended, hyphenated, or indigenous teachings sometimes have much in common.

This collection of essays, my spiritual legacy, blends ideas from the diverse viewpoints of students and friends who have graced me with their stories. The overarching theme of the collection is my own journey into the world of religious diversity and inclusion: my encounters with other answers, ideas, prompts, challenges, and resolutions. It is how I merged my concept of learning discernment with my personal search for answers to the existential questions which have meaning for me.

My stories came together in this collection like the stories told around the Thanksgiving table. Through our recollections, we remember, reunite, reassemble ourselves in community. Our departed ancestors and living relatives help us to identify ourselves within the tableau of our families. In religious liturgies, a similar kind of sacred storytelling happens to bring faith families together, remembering and reconnecting each week or holy day.

Spiritual storytelling invites us to listen to each other without making a list of arguments, refutations, or ways to persuade the speaker to think or believe differently. This is not a book of theological justifications; it is a collection of stories, which have given me a glimpse of our world. Though troubled, it seems to me that our world holds a promise filled with hope for the future.

Many of my stories form a memoir of my interfaith questions and interspiritual experiences, but they do more than offer an account of events. They are here because I am also called to teach or, at the very least, provide an opportunity for my readers to ask similar kinds of questions, engaging their imaginations. So, this is an ethical will, an interfaith journey, an imaginative venture, and a discernment guide—both memoir and an invitation to you to write your own answers, leaving your own spiritual legacy or ethical will to those who will follow you.

Like using the encyclopedias on the bookshelves in my childhood home, I hope my stories will inspire you to look beyond the pages and learn about yourself in new ways. Perhaps, it'll be like walking a labyrinth, turning in unexpected places, circling back a bit, returning, and renewing your journey. Each chapter includes questions for personal or collective exploration and ends with a prayer, poem, or spiritual meditation, like this one from the Shakers:

SIMPLE GIFTS

'Tis the gift to be simple, 'tis the gift to be free,
'Tis the gift to come down where we ought to be,
And when we find ourselves in the place just right,
'Twill be in the valley of love and delight.
When true simplicity is gained,
To bow and to bend we will not be ashamed,
To turn, turn will be our delight,
Till by turning, turning we come round right
©Public Domain

Melanie-Préjean Sullivan
September 2021; Days of Awe, 5782

Introduction

If you pay close attention, you will discover that wonders and mysteries
are hidden everywhere. . . we can find God's presence hidden everywhere because
God created everything. . . all things are connected to one another.
—Lawrence Kushner (*Spirituality*, 27–29)

I've collected stories all my life; it might be slightly genetic. My dad was a tremendous storyteller, both real stories and jokes. I don't think I ever heard him tell the same joke more than once. People on the Friday night busses to our high-school football games used to vie for a place on Dad's bus. Although I don't have his memory for jokes, I do remember good stories told to me, and I enjoy telling stories from my own experiences. Stories help me to find meaning in my life and to illustrate all kinds of concepts for teaching others.

Storytelling has been a part of all civilizations. Even before letters formed words, stories were recorded as sketches or pictograms thousands of years ago on the caves at Lascaux and the monuments in Egypt. Stories transmit collective memory, teach valuable moral lessons, create cohesive communities, and serve to help us to become our best selves.

Stories are an important part of relationships. When we hear others' stories, we come to know them, and when we share our stories, friendships happen. It is why storytelling is one of the key components of interfaith education, especially the work of the Interfaith Youth Core (IFYC). As I attended several of their annual Interfaith Leadership Institutes, I learned firsthand how very valuable it is for educators to help young adults sharpen their skills in the art of telling a good story. Those sessions helped me to identify the important stories in my own life.

You are approaching this collection for your own purposes, but I have assumed that one of those is to find a guide for grappling with life's ultimate questions. One way, the way I've chosen, is to collect stories from my past that I think provided my initial answers to such questions. I invite you to do the same: collect your stories and discover some answers that are waiting for you.

JOURNALING

We can collect those stories by journaling, regarded by many as an important tool for spiritual growth and development. For many years, I resisted the idea because I was afraid that I might write something in my journal that would be read after my death and be taken out of context, misunderstood, or worse, hurt someone's feelings. There was also more than a bit of ego wrapped up in that fear. I didn't want my family to think less of me when reading something I wasn't there to explain. For example, I have changed my mind over time about some important things, so writing a journal entry today might not reflect my resolution of the question in years to come. But I am working to push my ego out of the way because I often learn best by writing.

Libraries and bookstores have shelves of books with advice about journaling, and there are fancy journals to help you begin. I have only three suggestions: First, when you decide to purchase a journal, make it an inexpensive one. You don't want a beautiful leather-bound journal to sit on the shelf because it's too pretty to mess up. Second, make sure it is one without perforations. You don't want to tear out pages because sometimes the pages we regret writing are the *very* ones we should reread and analyze later. Finally, journal in ink. Again, you don't want to be tempted to erase something. A misspelled or misplaced word or phrase that seems out of place might be the very idea that needs your attention or reassessment.

MUSCLE MEMORY

When I taught discernment to undergraduates, I suggested that they journal each day, in a consistent place, and at about the same time. This was to help them create a muscle memory for their bodies to connect to their spirit. As a former study skills teacher, I had taught students not to study in bed because their bodies would think it was time to sleep. My discernment students found that their bodies *knew* it was time to journal after only a few days of practicing this new habit.

I assigned two questions to ask and answer each day: *For what are you most grateful today? For what are you least grateful?* I was trying to help them cultivate an attitude of gratitude, to see small places of grace in their days and glean hints about themselves. It helped them begin to answer their primary question of purpose. Most were discerning a career, graduate or professional school, or a vocation to religious life or ministry.

For my readers, I invite you to use the questions within each chapter to begin to create your own narrative, which might or might not include aspects of a daily discernment journal. Of course, the questions are only suggestions. As you get into the rhythm of reading the essays, you'll probably be able to anticipate the questions. At the very least, you'll be able to form the questions that you most need to ask yourself—no matter what I've asked you to consider.

Finally, one advantage of having these answers in a journal is that you'll easily be able to read back over your stories. I've found this helpful because I can be more objective with time between writing and rereading. This objective, almost like a second-person frame of mind, is especially helpful as we process our memories, both pleasant feelings and old hurts.

CATCHING UP

There is an inspirational story about a journey during the height of imperialism in Africa. A team of Europeans had enlisted the aid of several native guides for some purpose. They'd been walking for hours in the heat and humidity of a jungle, and suddenly the guides stopped. No amount of coaxing from the organizers of the journey could convince the natives to move. Finally, their translator explained that they had stopped because of the pace; they had stopped to *allow their spirits to catch up with their bodies.*

Isn't that the most wonderful way of expressing how we often feel? I know I've had to be reminded to slow down, to take a holiday, to stop acting like a workaholic, to spend time recharging my spiritual battery. My hope is that the process of reading and reflecting, which this book invites you to do, will help you to allow your spirit to catch up.

Within each of the chapters, I have collected essays around a theme. At various places within each chapter, I've inserted questions. They are ideas placed there deliberately to give you time to pause and consider what you have read, to see what the stories you've read have triggered in your own memory, and to give you something to ponder as you let your spirit catch up.

"GOD-LANGUAGE"

Speaking of spirits, we might mention the big one: the Holy Spirit of God. Some of my students who were from religious backgrounds had lots of experiences reading or thinking with "God-language." Others preferred to avoid any traditional God-language, but to think of a Sacred

Presence, a Divine Energy, the Creative Force, or some other name for the notion of the ultimate and great Other. Some preferred to leave the Other completely out of the conversation. If you are like those in this last category, I apologize; this book does not do that well. I have used lots of God-language, even while I desire to be as inclusive as possible.

Writing from one theological perspective to an audience that is diverse in religion, faith, and tradition is a daunting task. I cannot hope to serve all people equally. I am acutely aware that my Catholic Christian background is fraught with assumption problems, and that any attempts to speak of belief, faith, or even discerning answers to ultimate questions is limited. My Jewish friends caution about the way in which Christians use the word *faith* as indicative of *belief.* We need to remember there is no prescribed set of beliefs or creed in Judaism or in many other religions. Even the term *interfaith* is somewhat inadequate, but I hope it is easily enough understood by my readers.

From my perspective, many of life's ultimate questions imply a greater Being, a plan, and a place for all of us. For me, it is easiest to begin with the first question of defining what I mean by God. For those who are agnostic or atheist, I hope you'll still find the exercises helpful, as many of my students did, for discovering how much you think there is some force that helps us to define our own sense of purpose and life's meaning.

The earliest attempts to answer life's ultimate questions of meaning have become sacred texts or scripture. They are associated with religions and play an important role in one's identity within a faith community. Most of these scriptures were compiled and esteemed by men in the very distant past, so it is helpful to me that these scripture stories are being reassessed by many women scholars.

I'm one of those women who is reassessing much of what is in my own religious tradition. There are glimpses of this in my stories; I feel compelled to find women's perspectives in my study of theology. For example, I might use a feminine pronoun for God within our exercises. Language is powerful, but I have confidence that you are an intelligent reader and perfectly capable of translating my language into your own.

PRACTICE DISCERNMENT

The questions which follow the essays are not designed to have simple answers. You'll have to do some pondering, to practice *discernment.* I'm using that term to mean more than merely deciding. Some think of discernment as a spiritual gift, a particular skill, or a personality trait, that only a few people possess. I don't think it is that limited. There are elements of true discernment that can be learned and practiced over a lifetime, and they can be linked to our theologies, our understanding of how God is involved in our lives.

When I first began to study discernment for my doctoral work, a priest colleague told me that I had no right to attempt this subject. He seemed terribly distraught by the whole idea. He went on to explain that only those who were trained in Ignatian Spirituality had that right. Only Jesuits (members of the religious order founded by Ignatius of Loyola) who have had years of study in the *Spiritual Exercises of St. Ignatius* could call themselves experts in discernment. I, on the other hand, do not think that Jesuits have an exclusive claim to the term or the process.

I do acknowledge that Ignatius left us an amazing plan for discernment, especially for the ultimate question of lifelong vocations. Many of my friends in religious vowed life pursue spiritual direction within a 30-day silent retreat when they need to discern an important life choice (e.g., entering a religious order, studying for ministry or for ordination, leaving community life, etc.) The attitude of discernment I'm attempting to introduce in this book is not meant to substitute for spiritual direction or a retreat of such intensity.

Some of the ideas of Ignatius' *Spiritual Exercises* are critical parts of answering life's ultimate questions. Ignatian retreatants are asked to connect their feelings with their minds; they are encouraged to use their imaginations and to place themselves inside of stories from Scripture. They are encouraged to be in touch with their feelings of both *desolation* and *consolation* to help them to come to the right decisions. You might find hints of this process throughout the essays, but this is not a book on Ignatian spirituality.

IMAGINATION

The most challenging question for many of us who have been involved in practical theology or ministry is the question of the existence of suffering and evil. If God is Love, why is there such hate in our world or bad things happening to good people? I'm not sure I've ever found any theologian who has answered that question adequately, so I embark on the adventure of seeking comfort in *not-knowing*, and I have used the advice of other authors to assist me. There is a lot to be learned from this kind of thinking outside of the box.

One of the messages of my chaplaincy training was that we would be invited to journey with people who needed to make a leap or a change. The metaphor for ministry was one of attempting to free a vehicle in the mud, helping those in our spiritual care to become *unstuck* and to help them move into new ways of thinking, away from places which *bogged them down.* That often requires a bit of imagination, more thinking outside of the box. Thus, I encourage you to use your imagination, to recover your childlike sense of wonder, so that you can avoid places where you might be caught, unable to feel free.

Imaginary friends are part of one of my essays, but I do not equate imagination with the imaginary or fictious. Instead, I'm suggesting that you use your imagination, your talent for daydreaming, to find new ways of seeing things. Approach ideas from new perspectives so that you encounter creative possibilities.

A FRENCH PANTOUM

To engage my imagination and creativity, I created a French Pantoum, a poetic repetition of ideas. If you search online you will find various patterns, but the one I prefer is outlined in *The Artist's Rule* (Paintner, 77–9).

After journaling several pages, set them aside for a couple of days. When you reread them, circle six key phrases. On a blank page, rewrite the phrases, giving each a number and then arrange them in this pattern: lines 1, 2, 3, 4; 2, 5, 4, 6; and 5, 3, 6, 1.

During the pandemic, I was searching for Wisdom, so I arranged phrases from my journal. Here is the pantoum I created on that day:

> *Listen to what is said and unsaid*
> *Attend to Earth and her sacred message*
> *Hold Truth in esteem*
> *Remember who you are called to be*
> *Attend to Earth and her sacred message*
> *Daily choose to love*
> *Remember who you are called to be*
> *Rely on my help*
> *Daily choose to love*
> *Hold Truth in esteem*
> *Rely on my help*
> *Listen to what is said and unsaid*

It was a helpful summary of what I had journaled previously and what I knew the voice of Wisdom was trying to tell me. Months later, it still serves to remind me of the wisdom available to us, even when we do not notice it.

May you find joy in the journey.

An Apartment Next to the Angels

Assessing Our Theologies and Worldview

Before I formed you in the womb I knew you,
and before you were born I consecrated you.
—Jeremiah 1:5

Thomas Merton became famous after his spiritual autobiography, *The Seven-Storey Mountain* was published in *1948*. Written from within the rolling foothills of central Kentucky, the book caused his monastery to become a site of pilgrimage for tens of thousands each year. I am fortunate enough to live near the Abbey of Gethsemani and to have a couple of friends who like to take the easy drive down on a Sunday afternoon to pray Compline (Night Prayer) with the monks.

On one such trip in 1994, Fr. Matthew Kelty spoke to us after Compline, sharing a story from a radio interview about *A Book of Angels* by Sophy Burnham. The author had relayed the experience of a couple whose young daughter wanted to be left alone with her newborn brother. She was persistent while they were apprehensive. Finally, they placed a monitor in the crib, so she would think she was completely alone with him. They listened to the monitor from the hallway as their daughter tiptoed to the crib. In the quiet, she leaned over her newborn brother's crib and whispered, pleading, "Tell me about God; I'm forgetting."

The story stayed with me through the drive home, into my dreams that night, and into the following morning. As we drove to school, I decided to ask my 5-year-old son, Sean, if he remembered life before he was born. "Oh yes," he answered with great confidence, "I had an apartment right next to the angels." We drove a little longer, and he continued to tell me about what his life was like in heaven. Then, I asked him to tell me about God. "Well, God was like a bright light, but not so bright that it hurt your eyes. And God was warm, but not hot."

After another pause, I couldn't resist asking my final question which was whether God was a man or a woman. My young son, with the wisdom of a sage, was incredulous. His tone was a tad condescending when he said, "Mom! It was God!" At least he didn't say, "Stupid woman!" I could tell he was questioning my intelligence to suggest that God had gender.

If you know anything about me, you know that at that moment I was overjoyed. I had a son who did not think of God as an old king in the sky. He could think deeply, theologically, and with an openness that was a dream come true for me. He was delightfully articulate in explaining his experiences of heaven, angels, and God. To this day, his vivid descriptions keep me mindful of our connection to imagination and the Divine Spirit. And, to this day, he remains that deeply thoughtful, inclusively spiritual man. Thank you, God.

This notion of connection to a Divine Order from before we are born, through the blessings and tribulations of our earthly existence, and into an afterlife is a notion that never fails to sustain me with hope. When I first drafted this chapter, we were in the fourth week of social-distancing because of Covid-19, and I found it more challenging to think or to write creatively.

Outside, the sky was blue while the trees were losing their flowers and being replaced with that delicious shade of spring green leaves. The wind was blowing a cool breeze, and it was a gorgeous spring day. But, just a few miles away, people were dying of an invisible bug. A virus which showed only the proclivity to reproduce, was invading innocent people and destroying the most vulnerable of them. We sat isolated and healthy, but I knew this experience was filled with the same kind of message as the story I heard from the Abbey. We were forgetting about God in our fear and trepidation, in our blaming and anxiety.

When memories flood my mind, I know they are important. It's not just about an experience long ago. I'm supposed to learn something from the memories now. Perhaps it is because we are forgetting who and whose we are.

PONDER . . .
What favorite stories from your past remind you of your earliest notions of God?

WHAT IS YOUR THEOLOGY?

My son's recollection of his life in heaven before he was born is an illustration of his first theology, his first image of God. When I began teaching about discernment in the classroom, I wanted to introduce my students to the idea that each of them might have a picture of God, even if they had rejected it or felt they had outgrown it.

The class was entitled, "The Theology of Discernment," and it was an elective. So at least some of them were there because they really wanted to study the topic. I chose to begin each class with a prayer, a poem, or some sort of invocation asking for our minds and hearts to be opened. Students took turns reading either their own words or those of a favorite author.

Certainly, the idea of praying for the Spirit of God to assist in their discernment was problematic. For those who identified as agnostic or atheist, any instructions about praying might cause resistance or serve to block their capacity to engage the topic. I also didn't want to assume an unacceptable theological stance with those students who think of God as a chess player who moves pawns around on a board, with each of our steps mapped out for us.

In speaking about discernment, I also purposely avoided the use of the word, "sign" as if prayer would help them conjure up easy or quick answers to their serious questions about their futures. I realized that I needed to help students who regularly prayed, as well as those who had stopped praying, to think about to whom they prayed. I asked students who had never prayed or didn't believe in a God to indulge me in an exercise to serve as an introduction to thinking about theology, the ways in which God or gods have been defined. I created an imaginary situation to help them think about images of God. We called it, "Melanie the Martian."

First, we imagined that I was a space traveler who had landed upon the earth, who had been studying our little community for many years. Melanie the Martian decided to identify herself to us because she needed our help. Her assignment had been to master our language and she had done so with some success, but she couldn't figure out what we meant by the word, "god."

Next, I asked the students to try to help our little Martian friend and to write three nouns which would be the closest metaphor for what we think of, when or if we could imagine God, and to label them 1, 2, 3. They suggested words like "king, father, and friend." (Yes, most used male language.) Our Martian was still a bit confused by the metaphors, so she would ask us to further clarify with three descriptors; we would label them A, B, and C. They chose words like "loving, merciful, and powerful."

Melanie the Martian was now totally confused. We had told her that there is only one God, but we had just named nine! If you match each descriptor with each noun, you have nine descriptions (A-1, A-2, A-3, B-1, etc. or phrases like "loving king, loving father, loving friend; merciful king, merciful father," etc.)

Even though we might say we believe in only one God, those of us who pray, do so to different manifestations for different issues. We pray to an almighty presence when we want some "big" thing fixed. We pray to another kind of presence when we are sad or in pain. It isn't easy for a "monotheist" to admit, but when we engage in this kind of exercise, we can realize how many different pictures we have of God, with a capital G. (Islam lists 99 names for God; Judaism lists 70; Christians speak of a Trinity; but they are all names for what these faiths call the ONE.)

This is also an excellent time to explore some of the harmful and limiting nouns and descriptors floating in our psyches. If your god is a "judgmental bookkeeper" waiting for you to sin and mess up your life, you might not allow yourself to see God as a loving grandmother or gentle friend who offers you comfort when you are sad. If your image of a god is one who rewards you but sends your nonbelieving friends to hell, that is a god that you might find very difficult, if not impossible to love. "A stingy god is not a god for me," as a recent meme posited.

After this exercise, students would remark that they had suddenly realized how confusing their theologies were. It was often an aha moment for those who believed in God to begin to understand why many do not. It also helped to have a Jewish student who explained that YHWH is purposefully without vowels, so it cannot be pronounced because God cannot be limited. She explained how some Christian attempts to add vowels to the name to pronounce it made no sense to her; it wasn't God's real name with those vowels; it was something else.

When my students encountered terms like *power, majesty,* and *authority,* they seemed to find a hard contrast to the personification of God as unconditional love and care. Some thought of God as a gatekeeper or, even worse, an executioner. For many, all their images were male authority figures; others, pictured a grandmother or best friend. Some students also realized that it wasn't that they didn't believe in God, but that they had chosen not to believe in the god of the negative theologies from Sunday School.

We had long discussions about how we create our images of God to suit our needs and wants at any given time. These conversations were opportunities to offer a healing encouragement to those who had severely suffered from religious traditions that condemn nonbelievers or from preachers who engage in what I call, "ministerial malpractice."

PONDER . . .
If you encountered a Martian who wanted to know what you meant when you spoke about God, what nouns and adjectives would you use? Is there one that you listen to most often, pray to most fervently, or trust unconditionally?

BAPTISM IN A RIVER

When I was in my first semester of graduate theology, we were assigned a short story to read. It was about a baptism in a river. We were instructed to read only the story and not to attempt to look up anything else about the story for our homework that evening. The following day, instead of asking us about the story, our professor asked us to describe our images of the author. Was the author male or female? Was it likely that the author was from a particular region of the country? Could we tell anything about the faith of the author? He taught us to "look for clues" in the narrative, clues to tell us something about the theology of the author.

We learned to see how writers leave hints in their writing that reveal their opinions, perspectives, or origins. Just like the writer of the short story, theologians also leave such hints. Hints about who they are and what they believe are either very attractive to us or they are not. I think reading theology is sometimes like dating: You might read an author's work and think, "I do not intend to go out with him ever again!" Other times, you can't wait for another meeting.

The point of the exercise in that theology class was to help us realize that when we study theology, we are studying someone else's view of God. As we embarked on graduate study, we were going to encounter theologians whose work we loved or detested. Our assessment of the validity of the theology of any theologian, including the most well-respected within the Catholic tradition, was going to depend upon our own theologies. When I taught undergraduates, the same lesson was an important one for me to pass along to them.

The theology in Paul's epistles, in Augustine's *Confessions* or Aquinas' *Summa* were often the only theologies my Christian students knew. When I was able to introduce them to quotes from Elizabeth Johnson's *She Who Is*, it opened their eyes to a new paradigm. Especially for the young women, it created a space for them to feel valued in a different way and gave them a freedom they had never encountered. So, the first step along the road to discerning what God is calling us to be is to figure out *who* this God is that we think is calling us.

◇

PONDER . . .
What are the positive images of the Divine that match your theology? What is it about this God that you embrace?

Instead of reading theological texts in my first discernment course, we read spiritual quotes and segments of the psalms or other scripture passages and spiritual poems. We analyzed the ways in which some prayers ask for help from a God who loves us, while others are prayers of gratitude to a God whom we believe is powerful and protective. We discussed how our images of God can change over time and within some circumstances and how negative images of God (controlling, stingy, hypercritical) can affect or destroy our prayer lives. We considered how often we treat God as a "Divine Butler," summoning and dismissing God as we please.

When students were given permission to think about these images, given the freedom to accept or reject theologies that had been imposed upon them, new spiritualities emerged. On at least three occasions, students who had identified as atheist said that they wanted to believe in a different God than the one which had been given to them by the preachers and churches of their childhood, the ones they had rejected. Notice the idea they expressed as they *wanted to believe*. Here is a concept for us to ponder.

◇

PONDER . . .
Do I believe in the God I want to exist? Is faith actually desire? How is my prayer life affected by the writers of my favorite prayers, by their theologies?

A MARVELOUS BURNING BUSH

One of my favorite pastimes in recent years has been studying scripture with friends in a local synagogue. I've been invited to learn Hebrew along the way and to look at scripture passages that I might have taken for granted before. (In another essay, I will explore how we don't realize how much we've been told what to think/believe. It's hard to separate what a passage *says* from what we've been taught to believe it *means*.)

The story in Exodus 3:2–4 of Moses and the burning bush is a helpful way of looking at the first step in discernment. First, an angel appeared in the form of a flame, then it reads, "he looked, and the bush was blazing, yet it was not consumed." After this verse, it continues with Moses' remarks, "I must turn aside and look at this great sight and see why the bush is not burned up." The voice of God from the bush did not call out to Moses until he turned to look at it or as this translation continues, "he had turned aside to see." If you read carefully, you'll notice that not only did he look at it, but he looked with awe and amazement at how "great" the sight was. It can happen to us, when we are considering events in our lives, journaling our own essays. They cannot speak to us until we look and marvel at them. Inspiration, insight into discernment decisions, resolutions, and consolations are likely to occur when we spend some time gazing lovingly as we write our own stories, very carefully. We begin to see how marvelous they are, sometimes seeing them clearly for the first time.

In the Christian Greek Orthodox liturgy, there is a phrase which the priest uses before he reads from Scripture. He intones a solemn set of notes as he chants, "Let us be attentive." The Roman Catholic Church of my childhood used bells during Masses in Latin for the same purpose, to make sure we were paying close attention at the right times. I think the four words of the Orthodox and the bells illustrate the burning bush story and what it really means to be involved in discerning answers to important questions by paying attention.

———————————— ◇ ————————————

PONDER . . .
How do you invite yourself to be attentive? Have you ever stopped to marvel at something or someone, only to realize you were in the presence of the Sacred?

A MINDFUL AIRCRAFT CARRIER

Let's return to Melanie the Martian and the exercise about articulating our theology. Once we assert what we think about God with some degree of certainty, we need to find a way to deepen our relationship. We need to find a way to listen to God more and ask less, to stop treating God as a "Divine Butler," summoned and dismissed.

To deepen that relationship, many of us practice prayer or meditation, manifested in any number of forms. At the university where I worked, for new student orientation, we created a "boat exercise" to help illustrate different types of prayer and how they are linked to our personalities. We wanted to emphasize the ways in which different people pray and that those differences cross religious and denominational lines.

We read descriptions of four different types of spiritualities and used different boats to correspond to each label. Then, we had students gather into their boat group to discuss what they enjoyed most about that type of prayer or connection to the Sacred. Those with a *sailboat* spirituality found connection to the Sacred in nature and silence, in stillness and awareness of the present and all that was happening around them. Those who found their greatest connection to God by helping others, in service, or working for social justice might be *tugboats*. *Cruise ship* spiritualities found God in music and dance, in large groups like a praise or charismatic event. Finally, *aircraft carriers* delighted in schedules and order; they found comfort in prayer forms that are written or memorized like liturgies in a prayer book.

The first time we did this exercise, I joined the group of fellow aircraft carriers to explain how much I liked praying morning and evening prayers with the Benedictine Sisters or Monks and how I use a prayer book for both my morning and night prayers each day. It meant that I was praying "with" thousands of women and men all over the world. One of our students in the group is now a rabbi. He was able to share similar elements of my story, that he enjoyed praying with others in *Minyan*, the gathering of at least 10 for morning and evening prayers, using a prescribed order of prayers and a prayer book.

Over time, people try different types of prayer styles. Our little boat exercise was to help students discover their "default" style, but they quickly realized that life would be much more interesting if they explored other styles from time to time. For some, the practice of centering prayer helps them to clear their minds of the extraneous and allow God's voice to be heard. For others, there are practices of mindfulness.

Mindfulness can be sitting quietly in silence for 20 or more minutes each day (maybe like a sailboat). For me, mindfulness is increasing my awareness of the presence of God by letting go of the questions and simply performing some repetitive tasks. One of my friends loves to iron as part of her spiritual practice. I take regular walks each morning, but I also enjoy washing the dishes. When I put on my yellow gloves and create hot, soapy water, I relax and move into a lovely zone of contemplation. I place all my attention on the process of cleaning and rinsing each plate and pan. When they are settled in the drying rack, I carefully wipe the counters and the stovetop. I clean the sink, rinsing the dishcloth several times in the hot, running water to remove all the soap. When I've finished, there is a sense of completion, of leaving the kitchen ready for the next meal, and my mind is clear. There is a tremendous sense of finishing and starting over, like mercy and forgiveness after a rough patch.

PONDER . . .
Using a boat as metaphor for your spirituality, what is your default preference for finding spiritual connections? How have you found peace and connection with your spiritual self and/or the Sacred Presence?

ARCHITECT OR HOSTESS

After you have come to some conclusions about your personal images of God and of how you make connections to these images, you might begin to ask yourself how you think God works in the world. This idea is associated with what some call a worldview (rather than a religion). It explains how you think your life and the universe itself unfold.

For instance, do you picture yourself approaching God in a board room where there is a huge table upon which is placed the blueprint for your life? Is God like an architect who hands you the blueprint and expects you to act as a compliant builder who executes the plan, constructing the infrastructure and edifice of your life?

Or is God a "Sacred Hostess" who meets with you periodically to hand you an invitation? Over your lifetime, She issues many such invitations to attend something after which you have choices about accepting or rejecting them. No matter how many times you reject one invitation, God will never stop inviting you to consider a new path or new idea.

Perhaps, it's all much more closely related to chaos theory. Everything is random and nothing is part of any plan. There is no predictability about what choices will appear or what the impact of our decisions will be. Even for many of us with a faith-based worldview, there might still be an element of the chaos or a random theory in our minds.

This can feel very overwhelming, a bit like the opening scene from the old *Mission Impossible* TV series, "Your mission, should you decide to accept it is. . ." I always wondered what kind of person would accept a mission which was impossible. Was it someone with a death wish or an egotist who never doubted him or herself? My theology of who or what God is has always been directly tied to how God works with me and for me in the world. It has always been a confident sense that I would never be abandoned, no matter what choices I made. I see God as a generous parent whose only "will" for me is a desire for my happiness and flourishing. More importantly, my theology tells me that nothing I might feel called to do will be impossible.

PONDER . . .
Do you believe that there is only one path for you, established before you were born and that your happiness depends upon you choosing that "right" one? Do we all have one soul mate, a single vocation, or set path for our lives that we must discern?

SEARCH FOR TRUTH

After we think for a while about the meaning of faith, we begin to think about what we mean by truth. The motto of the university where I served in campus ministry, was "in the love of truth." It was a phrase from an original prayer on the feast of Robert Bellarmine. It meant something to the founders, that students and faculty would not only love truth, but that they would be "in love" with it—infatuated, preoccupied, consumed by it.

Truth means different things to different people. Philosophers define it one way; theologians might agree or modify it. I have always found it challenging to work with people who think they have all the truth, that it is contained in a single bible verse or in one faith or institution. Part of the drive I've had to write this book rests in some internal desire to know or uncover the truth about what I believe. But I also recognize that I will never be able pin down everything I think is true.

For instance, I am confident in my observations of the world indicating the notion that God loves variety. As the psalmist writes, each of us is "fearfully and wonderfully made" (Psalm 139:14); thus, I believe that we are all unique gifts of God. Of course, some people are more interested in finding what they think is the ultimate "Truth" in a faith journey and others adhere to a religion because they are looking for community and connection. The latter I find comforting. Those whose search for truth has led them to certainty are not usually people I find particularly pleasant to be around me.

THE WISTERIA AND THE ROSE

One such encounter might illustrate what I mean by overconfident holders of truth. I have had the privilege of being associated with an institute founded for the education of Catholic women in Cambridge, England. In addition to courses, the institute sponsors educational programs and events, open to women and men, and to people of all faiths. One evening, we hosted a book-launch for an author who was a special friend, a fellow Catholic chaplain. After his talk, we had a typical Cambridge reception where many engaged either in more academic questions or in casual conversation with a glass of wine or juice in hand.

After picking up a glass, I turned around to find I was being approached by a man in a Roman collar who told me that the author featured in our gathering had referred him to me to answer a question. He asked me how I could justify interfaith work. His tone indicated to me that he was ready for a debate, maybe even a fight. I wasn't interested in that. "Justify" is a loaded word, filled with antagonism and a suggestion that my opinion was wrong, even though I hadn't answered his question. It indicated that he knew the truth.

The space in which we were gathered had windows and doors overlooking the most remarkable English garden. I turned to the closest window and pointed to the trees, bushes, and flowers in a magnificent vista of plants of all colors and hues. I said that I couldn't imagine a God who loved such variety in nature to be one who created all of us to be the same. The wisteria didn't try to convince the rose that she was the wrong plant! To me, the view of the garden seemed ample proof that God celebrates creation's diversity. Why would diverse religions be any less a part of that celebration?

He was not at all happy with my remarks. He wanted to engage all his energy in a theological debate. I wanted to scream, to run away. He began to lecture me on my insufficient opinion. I began to pray for someone to save me from this perfectly awful situation. My experience has taught me that you cannot otherwise persuade people who are convinced that their opinion is the only valid one. This was a no-win situation. Fortunately, just as my patience was nearly worn away, someone called our attention to thank the speaker again and to close our evening. I have rarely felt such gratitude for the end of an event!

PONDER . . .
Have you ever had to "justify" your belief to someone who judged your opinions as wrong or your arguments as insufficient? Where did you find the confidence to hold your ground?

Many of the exercises or questions I present to readers throughout this book are ones to be used for an individual to journal. They can also be used to prompt conversations in groups. Even if you choose to use the book for individual journaling, I think it is wise to mention here that sometimes we need someone to journey with us, to help us to clarify what we seem to be saying.

I recommend rereading your journal periodically to see what you might be repeating or writing unconsciously. It can be helpful to share your entries with someone to help you see what you might not be noticing. I've had the privilege of being such a companion to many in the past few decades, and I will share one or two favorite ones, which illustrate the gift that such companionship brings.

At the end of each academic year, the university celebrates Commencement weekend with a Baccalaureate Mass. The tradition includes three or four brief reflections from students at the end of the liturgy. I had the privilege of choosing students for this task, and I always tried to have diverse voices—differences in age and gender, religious affiliations, major fields of study, etc.

One year, I asked one of our Jewish students to deliver a reflection. Ari began by explaining that he had chosen a Catholic university deliberately because he wanted to learn from a different viewpoint. He closed by asking, "Where, but here, could a Jewish student discern his call to rabbinical school with a Catholic campus minister?" Years later, I was asked in an interview to relate my favorite moment in ministry; his was the story I told. Who could have imagined that I would receive such a gift, such an affirmation, that I was his interfaith chaplain, his spiritual companion?

On another occasion, a group of Druid and Pagan students asked me to help them find a place on campus to hold a ritual to welcome a new season. They needed to use real candles, so we needed a safe place outdoors. I suggested the grotto, a concrete area behind our Chapel close to a statue of Mary in a recessed niche. We secured permission from Campus Safety, and they held their ritual. The following week, they reported their experience to the Campus Ministry Council, student leaders from all the faith groups. One of the Catholic students made a face that indicated she was displeased with the beginning of the report. She quickly changed her demeanor, however, when the Druid student reported, "Of course, before we began our ritual, we thanked the Blessed Virgin Mary for allowing us to use her space." Her report had used a very Catholic term to indicate a level of reverence, beyond mere respect for our tradition. There was grace in that room which can never be described fully. As her spiritual companion, we had learned much from each other.

When I first researched discernment, I was thinking rather narrowly about helping Catholic students discern religious vowed or ordained life. I never imagined I'd have the privilege of walking with students who are now rabbis, ministers, priests, monks, imams, and sisters. I've learned from cradle Pagans, Unitarians, and many branches of Western and Eastern religions. Such a joy is interfaith chaplaincy! Seeing the face of God in young people from all faiths and none—watching them grow into theologians and physicians, ministers and musicians, botanists, and broadcasters. My students—my spiritual companions—brought me gifts without measure.

---------------◇---------------

PONDER . . .
Who have been your spiritual companions? To whom do you turn with your most pressing questions? Have you made room for those who might have different answers that would broaden your perspective?

Discernment is not a "one and done" process. It is a lifelong commitment to listening to the voice of the Divine or to the inspiration we name within our own spirituality or belief system. When we pause to listen, to observe, and to marvel as Moses did, the burning bush continues to speak to us. My interview with my young son about life with the angels invited me to try to pay attention to connections in the everyday and in the now.

All my life, I've learned as much—if not more—from people of faith traditions other than my own. I realized that their ultimate questions and mine were the same. I learned that the human inclination for asking the questions of why or what were ones we all shared and that a variety of answers was comforting. I could not insulate myself within my Catholic identity; I needed to reach out and to find new answers and connections.

My journey with individuals of all faiths and none has been one which continuously brings me to "an apartment next to the angels." Interreligious work does that. It connects us to people who are more than their creeds. We witness or are invited to participate in rituals that touch our spirit and remind us of the human-Divine connection to all of creation. The sounds of the shofar, waters of baptism, oil of confirmation, candlelight of Shabbat, bread and wine in Seder or Mass, and delicious dates to break the fast at Iftar are gifts of the earth, harvested and formed by human hands for the life of the world. This has been part of my interspiritual journey, reminding me of our connectedness and mutual call to make the world a better place because we are in it.

JAZZ AND JUSTICE

In the midst of nature, centuries-old sequoia trees don't wear watches. White-water rapids never even hear the Westminster chimes of the clock that sits on my bookshelf. Birds whistle, chirp, and call in their own rhythms, like my son playing his bass. When I see his eyes, lost in the moment—a gentle touch on a taut, strong string is a heartbeat in the background of the jazz tunes. It is strength personified, supporting the other instruments. When he plays jazz, it is a spiritual union that we witness: the beat of the heart of a man, of the earth, the universe, the rhythm of God.

Sometimes when we are attentive to such times, we experience great joy. Other times, we can see where we have fallen short of all we hoped to do and be. As I wrote the first draft of this essay, many voices in the news claimed that the world economy was in jeopardy as our consumerism came to a screeching halt. Just as Merton wrote in his journal so many times, our culture (like an insatiable virus) has been eating away at the "true self" God designed each of us to become. Merton wrote about the evils of racial injustice and had many readers and followers, but many of us have forgotten to continue to respond to this call. Due to the virtual meetings required during the Covid-19 pandemic, many who had never had friends of another race, creed, or gender identity now count their blessings with diverse friendships. Perhaps that is progress.

Perhaps, but the system is still not a just one. People still are judged by their religion, the color of their skin or their ethnic accents, by their sexual orientation or zip code, or their bank accounts, rather than by their character. Deepening our spirituality includes encountering the invitation to do something about this inequity, to confront injustice, to make a difference. The system needs to be changed, and we are part of that initiative, each in our own way.

I think our progress on justice issues has stalled because we are forgetting. When we had our apartments next to the angels, we knew that God loved us and all of creation. We understood beauty and generosity. We felt the warmth of God's presence and basked in the light of connection. As we continue in our journey to ask important questions, we look for the places where we have made progress and the places where we have fallen short of all God hopes us to be.

PONDER . . .

Pause for a moment to remember, to stop forgetting. Look over your responses to the question of your earliest notion of God. What helps you to recall that notion and to respond to the call to be a unique presence in the world, to be your true self?

Sacred Presence,
We call you by many names: Adonai, Christ, Allah,
Great Spirit, Shekinah, Brahma, Krishna (add your own).
Through your many manifestations, despite our limited understanding,
you never leave us. Even when we forget,
you guard and guide us in ways we may not see.
Help us to be more aware of your presence,
to honor your call with our careful response.
Amen.

2

Grandfathers Who Drive Studebakers

Beginning a Spiritual Autobiography

I think somehow, we learn who we really are
and then we live with that decision.
—Eleanor Roosevelt

When I recall stories from my past, I like to recall as many details as possible. It helps me to add dimension to them, to remember them with greater clarity. Famous people write their autobiographies to add details to the stories they think people only know in glimpses from news articles or tabloids. For discerning answers to life's ultimate questions, there is a different type of autobiography, a spiritual autobiography.

SPIRITUAL AUTOBIOGRAPHY

One of the most rewarding parts of the course I designed to teach college students about discernment was reading their first spiritual autobiographical essays. They seemed to pour such positive energy into the exploration of how they had first conceived of God or their connection to something greater than themselves.

The exercise that I learned and passed on to them about writing that essay began with recalling the sights, sounds, and smells of our earliest positive memories. They could have been outside or indoors, at home or on vacation. One might recall a family reunion, another, a quiet evening at home with parents. Once we have engaged those senses and traveled back in time, we can examine our spirituality in context. We repeat the sensory recollection at different ages along our timeline, asking the same questions or examining the same ideas until we reach our current age.

STEEN'S SYRUP POPCORN BALLS

Cinnamon-pecan oatmeal cookies, cornbread dressing, cold tomatoes sliced next to warm rice and gravy, peppermint sticks, summer squash with vanilla, and seafood gumbo simmering on the stove—these are more than recipes from my Cajun childhood; they are vivid memories which transport me back to another time and place. I use them when I'm trying to remember important stories from my past, stories which form part of my spiritual autobiography. Writing this list helps me to analyze my journey and to see the intersections, especially where I made choices.

You also might recall your favorite memories of comfort food, as you examine photos from your childhood. It might help you to recall feelings you had on a particular day. Many of my photos are in a pink baby book with black pages on which Mom wrote captions in white ink. Only one loose Polaroid photo tucked into the back of the book was taken at a time I remember.

The photo is of me with my best friend, my sister Andrea on the day of her First Communion. She was seven and I was nine. She wore her white dress and lovely veil. I was wearing my ninth birthday gift: a nun's habit.

I wonder how many Catholic girls used bath towels on their heads when they were pretending to be nuns, playing school on rainy days at home. Apparently, my mom grew tired of the little holes that the safety pins wore into our towels, so my grandmother sewed a little habit for me—black dress, detached white wimple, white forehead band, and black veil. Years after I outgrew the dress, I was still wearing the headband and veil to play school or army hospital in the grove of pine trees behind our grandparents' house. There were seven of us, always enough for pretending. Board games were for other families; we played *pretend*.

Using memories of your favorite foods and photos can be effective ways of remembering. When we recall our most pleasant memories, we have a glimpse of our true selves. Then we are prepared to ask ourselves the questions that reconnect us to our growing awareness of God and our relationship.

———————————— ◇ ————————————

PONDER . . .
What do your memories tell you about who you thought you were or who you would become?

TRUSTWORTHY MEMORIES

A word of caution: Make sure that the memories are really your memories and not something someone has told you about an event. For example, there was a story told about me at almost every extended family gathering until I was old enough to plead for people to stop telling the story.

Apparently, I was about 3 years old wearing my favorite dress, riding in the passenger seat of my grandfather Préjean's Studebaker. I do remember the car—a sporty, cream-colored two-door with brown horsehair carpet. The year was probably 1956, so there were no seatbelts to hold me in place.

As we were driving along, another car ran a stop sign, forcing my grandfather to break suddenly. I went shins forward sliding on the horsehair carpet to stop under the dash. When he asked if I was okay, I stood up and brushed the dust off my dress, propped my left hand firmly on my hip and shook my right hand. Pointing a finger in admonishment, I said, "Grandfathers who drive Studebakers should not slam on their brakes when their granddaughters are in the car!"

Those who know me today would likely be quick to agree that I haven't changed much at all. Though you might not use the word, *precocious* to describe my adult self today, it is evident that I am still extremely confident that I know what is right and wrong. To me, it still only makes sense that one demand justice where it is not. There are codes of behavior I expect people to follow without question, and I expect intelligent people to make good decisions.

That story, however, is not really mine to tell because I don't remember much about that incident. I have a very faint memory of the way my little shins must have ached later that day, but I don't remember talking to my grandfather like that, only his telling and retelling of the story with comical imitations of my outrage.

So, while stories about us may be helpful in our recollections, a spiritual autobiography needs to use our real memories, perceptions, and feelings to be authentic. When we recall the smell of our grandmother's sachet, we can transport ourselves back to a time of comfort or happiness. When we engage with that little self in the old photo, we can try to remember what we thought about God.

PONDER . . .

How did your image of God change through your childhood?

FEARLESS IMAGINATION

I think writing a spiritual autobiography is very rewarding because it reveals connections we might have forgotten. As children, we are often more in touch with the world and its rhythms. Our imaginations take flight. We encounter wonder when we see a butterfly or listen to a mourning dove. We play with words and ideas, away from the pressure of school assignments. Life is blessing, and we know it.

Unfortunately, there is this welcome place for imagination in our earliest years that many of us are forced to lose. I write *forced* because I think that the most gifted artists are constantly forced to make a living in careers they would rather not have. In the twenty years I served in university chaplaincy, nearly every semester brought me into conversations with students who were being told to give up their dreams so they could earn a "proper living." My heart would break to hear the kinds of conversations their parents had with them, the threats of removing financial assistance, the fear that was rampant in those confrontations.

Sometimes I'd use those fear-filled talks to illustrate a point in another setting. When it was time for elections, I'd tell students to listen for the fear mongering in the adverts like, "Candidate X wants to take away all of your social security benefits and give them to undeserving immigrants." I'd say, with an appropriate level of indignation in my tone, "For heaven's sake! Can't you see that the person who wrote this ad is deeply disturbed and trying to make granny vote for his candidate, even if he is a lying, cheating, disgrace to the political arena? Really! Wake up, people. Fear is a four-letter word and using it to manipulate others is a disgrace!"

The outraged 3-year-old comes through! Where is God's spirit in this story? How can we look back on our lives and attempt to recapture the sense of adventure we felt as children? Some of us used our imaginations effectively, and they even stretched us to have imaginary companions, as J. Bradley Wigger explores in *Invisible Companions*. He writes of "see-through knowing" and quickly points to *Alice in Wonderland* before his amazing conversations with many children he interviewed. Reading his book invited me to remember my imaginary friend. Her name was "Miss Kadie," and she lived in Kalamazoo, Michigan.

Just to clarify, I lived in southwest Louisiana, over a thousand miles from Michigan. I knew no one from north of Shreveport, so where did Kalamazoo originate in my imagination? All I remember is that she was a wise friend, several years my senior, hence her title: *Miss*. She accompanied me on many an adventure in the wilds of our backyard, through wisteria vines and under the shade of great pecan trees. She encouraged me to climb a mulberry tree, but I didn't get very far. She gave me the courage to try a persimmon and often helped me create scrumptious new recipes for otherwise plain mud pies. Miss Kadie was wonderful.

My imaginary friend who embodied my imagination is just as much a part of myself as my sense of outrage at injustice; each is only one aspect of who I am. I can be very loving and forgiving, even if I do not suffer fools gladly. I have an extremely compassionate side and chaplaincy training (CPE or clinical pastoral education) helped me to discover and grow that aspect of myself. CPE helped me to integrate my thoughts and beliefs, my psychological studies with theology and spirituality. With such new perspectives, I came to understand how I was moving into a spiritual journey, which would take me far beyond the church in which I grew up. In writing my own spiritual autobiography, I used important intersections in my life to ask questions about myself and my beliefs.

⸺⸺⸺⸺⸺ ◇ ⸺⸺⸺⸺⸺

PONDER . . .
Did you have an imaginary friend? What were her or his attributes that made for such a good friendship? How did that friend give you courage to face your fears?

FIRST WORLDVIEW

When I was completing a course in business management, there was an assignment on intergenerational workplaces and the theory that our perception of the world is formed when we are about 10 years old. It was an impressive assignment, one I now find perfect to use when teaching discernment, to consider the state of the world (especially significant events) and attempt to analyze your reaction to it. I will use my own story as an example.

John F. Kennedy was assassinated when I was 10. I remember the controversy about the findings of the Warren Commission and the dispute about the "lone gunman." (My dad purchased the printed version of the proceedings, and I read through them with commitment.) I was deeply affected by the news coverage of Jim Garrison, the District Attorney in New Orleans who uncovered a wider conspiracy, and in my essay for the management course, I realized how greatly these events had influenced my worldview.

Until I wrote that essay on the world from the eyes of a 10-year-old, I didn't realize how deeply engrained that experience was. If men in authority in our own government conspired to kill Kennedy (which I naturally assumed had to do with our shared religion and his civil rights work), then who could be trusted? I realized how much I questioned authority. It was more than a rebellious stage for me; it was and continues to be a large part of my worldview.

My distrust of authority doesn't take me to massive conspiracy concerns, but it does mean that I have little respect for men with titles, unless I think they've earned them. I have found myself thinking of board members as a "bunch of suits, without a clue." How uncharitable I can be!

This has given me a perspective to consider in writing my spiritual autobiography because authority is connected to all kinds of faith statements. Whether it is Scripture and its translators or Church authority, I'm prone to ask for proof. I rarely accept the "teaching authority" of anyone without sound support and a plethora of footnotes. Even with those footnotes, I am not easily persuaded.

It's helpful in thinking about intergenerational work to consider the world of people around us. My understanding of my own lack of respect for authority and refusal to accept easy answers or the status quo mirrors those of my generation who protested the war in Vietnam and who marched for the Equal Rights Amendment. My mother-in-law was about 10 during the Great Depression. She washed and saved plastic bags, just in case. When I was a high-school counselor, many of my former students who were 10 during the first Desert Storm voluntarily enlisted in the military in record numbers. (Their Vietnam-era parents were dismayed.) My students who were 10 on September 11, 2001, have a view of the world falling apart that is impossible to discount.

My spiritual self is anchored in my 10-year-old self, as if there is a very, very long rope attached to that anchor, which has not prevented me from floating afar and gaining vastly new perspectives. It's led me to approach my retirement with some firm convictions about the need for interspiritual thinking. Remembering our past doesn't have to bind us. I think it might keep us tethered just enough to treasure the present and to have hope in our future.

PONDER . . .
What significant events occurred in the world when you were 10? How might your perception of them have formed or affected your worldview?

TIMELINE

As you begin to write your spiritual autobiography, you can ask and answer questions about your worldview and your spiritual life. You might notice how your beliefs changed or shifted about God, your religious tradition, rules, and rituals. Hints appear to reinforce what I first read as a teenager in the book of Sirach, "Happy is the person who meditates on wisdom and reasons intelligently, who reflects. . . on her ways and ponders her secrets" (14:20–21).

You might also create a spiritual legacy diagram on which you note the family members, friends, and teachers who might have helped you to form the spiritual dimension of yourself. What characteristics of your spiritual identity were first suggested by these mentors? For instance, I remember Dr. Betts in my first graduate program who told me that I had a natural gift for teaching. He knew that I dreamed of working in the museum field, but he still planted the seed that became a blooming plant in my later life. I thought of him every time I wrote a self-evaluation of my effectiveness in teaching a course.

You might also discover theologies or beliefs that you have totally abandoned and remember individuals who helped you let go and heal from negative images of the Divine. A student came into my office one day in tears. She said she couldn't understand a god who would take her grandmother away and leave her so despondent. She couldn't understand how anyone could believe in such a cruel god. I told her that I agreed with her. A cruel god wasn't one I'd believe in, either.

Stunned, she asked me to explain myself. We spent some time discussing my theology of a loving God who cries with us, who set the world and the laws of physics and anatomy in motion and never interferes with those laws or our free will. I explained that the motorist who chose to drink plus the weight of the automobile in motion that he chose to drive logically led to an accident, and unfortunately to her grandmother's death. I told her that I didn't believe God had caused her death. But I did and still believe God was weeping with her, sad for her loss as well as for the anguish that the driver must also be feeling. What happened in his life that made him drink so much and make such an awful decision? It's complicated, I know. Such occasions call us to serious thinking, rather than allowing us to be reductionists or to accept simplistic cause-and-effect answers.

PONDER . . .
Where have you encountered fears and anger in your life and tied those emotions to your thoughts about God and yourself in the world? How did you reconcile any disparities?

Each of us has received special gifts and talents. Our family of origin is one place we discover them. I happen to be the typical eldest daughter who thinks her dad was a genius. In fact, there were many conversations that reinforced my childhood hero-worship, after I was an adult. One of those was when he showed me a diagram of the seven of us: his children. He had sketched himself and drawn a line from his head, hands, etc., to our names.

Dad told me that when he wanted to have an intellectual discussion (head) about something he'd read, he usually asked me first. If he needed a heart decision, he consulted Andrea. When he wanted to laugh and relax, he called Rachell. To remind him of the beauty of God's creation and align his conscience, he looked to Renée. For artistic designs, he went to Mark; for building something, to John. To analyze something, he consulted Matt. Each of the seven of us matched a part of his being, and I think that God works the same way. It isn't that I couldn't also design something artistic or another one of us wouldn't want to discuss something we'd read. It was just a *default* place to start.

With many of our choices in life, when we want to move beyond our default, we think of the test of Goldilocks. Is it too cold, too hot or, "just right"? In many ways, I think that I've encountered other faiths in the same way that my dad connected us to his needs or Goldilocks tried out the porridge. I've witnessed Jewish students who started asking questions of their Buddhist roommates, only to discover the contemplative tradition within their own Judaism. I've known nonliturgical Christians who were attracted to Catholic rituals, but not all the Roman Church's teachings, so they found the Episcopal Church to be just right.

One student shunned by her parish when she came out as transgender discovered welcome in the Baha'i community. A Catholic converted to Judaism because it was "like coming home." My Muslim colleagues opened their homes to my students after 9/11 to build a sense of solidarity against terrorism. In a dozen trips to India, at an interfaith ashram founded by a Catholic priest and a Hindu priest, we were served a simple meal after we discussed the world's religions and their common goals. We prayed together in their prayer room.

My colleague in ministry, Fr. Ron used to say, "We don't welcome you because *you* are Catholic; we welcome you because *we* are Catholic." In other words, he connected the primary definition of catholic (universal) as a gospel call for Catholics to practice radical hospitality. In Greek, *kata holos* means "according to the whole." There is no place for an us-versus-them effect within our holistic understanding of *Catholic*.

PONDER . . .

Have you ever encountered the Sacred in a house of worship or a ritual other than your own? Describe what happened and what senses were involved (sight, sound, smell) in your full experience?

BARE FEET AND COVERED HEADS: FROM INDIA TO ISRAEL

Many of my most profound experiences of interfaith and interspiritual encounter have been within just a few miles of where I work or live. I am grateful for being a resident of Louisville, home to numerous groundbreaking interfaith agencies and events. I've been within a few yards of the Dalai Lama on two occasions, and I've been honored by his Tibetan monks twice with the gift of a white ceremonial *Khata* or stole as their symbol of honor, gratitude, and our unity of purpose. These were moving, and they left me speechless.

I've also had the gift of travel three times to visit the Franciscans of Kerala, India, to experience their hospitality. Superlatives are hardly adequate to describe the way we were welcomed there. We visited Hindu Temples and Christian shrines of all sorts. We had tea and cakes in the homes of Muslims and attended Catholic Mass in the local language, Malayalam. Upon arrival on each porch, we removed our shoes; we were entering a home, a place of worship, a place of holiness. We bowed with our hands together and said, "Namaste," which means "the God within me greets the God within you."

In the summer before the pandemic, I visited Israel. It was a trip facilitated by generous donors to thank me for the work I had done with a local synagogue. I was the only Catholic on the study trip of biblical sites, but I was treated as a sage for two of our site visits. I was invited to teach at Mt. Tabor during our visit to the Church of the Transfiguration and again at the Inn of the Good Samaritan. Each time I had the opportunity to share what I'd learned from the gospels in or very near the place depicted in those stories.

While we studied in Israel, I wore a *kippa* on my head out of respect for the scripture passages we studied. On Friday evenings, I prayed and sang in the synagogue and had the chance to observe fully two *Shabbatot* (Sabbaths) in Jerusalem. I led morning meditations a few times, leaving me feeling even more included and appreciated. Being in Israel felt like home, at some visceral level.

Even more inclusive, our Rabbi Bob and his wife, my friend Deborah, had a surprise ready for me. At the closing of our first Sabbath, *Havdalah,* they announced that they were going to accompany me to Mass the next day. I was touched. It wasn't something I'd expected, but I was so happy to have the chance to share my tradition.

Others from our study group joined us, and when we arrived, the Sacristan (organizer for the Mass) asked me if I would read the *Prayer of the Faithful*. So, I ended up participating in the liturgy and helping my Jewish friends follow along, as they recognized many familiar gestures and prayers from their own rituals. In answer to my personal prayers, the priest delivered a homily filled with messages of welcome and hospitality.

PONDER . . .
Have you ever witnessed the experience of prayers and rituals, through the eyes of visitors to your tradition? Have you ever covered your head or removed your shoes (even metaphorically) when you knew you were standing on holy ground?

FINAL THOUGHTS

Grandfathers who drive Studebakers without seatbelts should not slam on their brakes while their granddaughters are in the car. Sometimes we need to remember who we are, in all our feistiness and our sense of justice. We need to find our best selves and the parts we wish did not exist. We need to attempt to tell our stories with objectivity and compassion for ourselves and those who have been with us on the journey through life.

When memories weave into stories that address our spiritual thoughts and our questions about God or faith, they become spiritual autobiographies. In turn, our spiritual autobiographies can become our spiritual legacies, what we leave for those who will follow us. In the next chapters, we'll continue this journey through memories, new questions, and a few challenges.

Blessed are you, O God, Creator and Sustainer of our being.
Thank you for the gift of life, for the gift of those in my life who love me,
and for the gifts and talents you have given me.
Help me to know myself as you know me, to live up to
your expectations, to reach my full potential for the good of all I meet.

3

Ginger Cakes in a Brick Oven

Collecting Memories; Remembering Mentors

Be who God meant you to be and you will set the whole world on fire.
—St. Catherine of Siena

Whenever there is a tragic event, it is said that you will always remember with meticulous detail exactly where you were, when you heard about the event. For example, I remember that I was on the telephone, ordering my first mobile phone on the morning of September 11, 2001. Someone ran into the office to tell me to report immediately to a university-wide assembly. I also remember that it was raining on November 22, 1963, because we were inside instead of outside at recess, when we were told that President Kennedy had been shot.

Besides tragedies, sometimes an important event in our lives is imprinted with the same precision and detail. Just so, I remember the fragrance of ginger cakes coming out of the brick oven at Colonial Williamsburg because it was in that village of living history where I decided I wanted to be an historian. The taste of ginger always transports me back to that warm afternoon, eating in the shade. I was 13 years old.

On that same family vacation to Virginia, there was one night when the babysitter wasn't available. I wasn't quite old enough to care for all my six siblings and five cousins, so my uncle volunteered to stay home, while the other adults went out. After the others had fallen asleep, he allowed me to "stay up" for a serious conversation about my future. He explained all about college and choosing a major; he told me about graduate school, about academic degrees—bachelors, masters, and doctorates. On that night, with the memory of costumed docents and the taste of ginger cakes still fresh in my mind, I decided that I wanted to earn a doctorate.

Throughout my undergraduate years, I remember "knowing" that I would continue to graduate school. I didn't discern it carefully; I took it as a given. For years, I thought it would be a PhD and that I would spend three to five years specializing in some topic of history. When I finally arrived at the University of Kentucky to pursue studies in English history, the dream was becoming less concrete. I was starting to doubt my abilities.

IMPOSTER SYNDROME

Surrounded by dozens of seemingly brilliant doctoral students, I was intimidated. I couldn't read and retain as much as they seemed to retain. ("Imposter syndrome" was not yet a common concept.) Also, I wasn't sure what I was going to be able to do with a doctorate in English history besides teach. As much as I enjoyed the classroom, I could not imagine myself there for the rest of my life. I had imagined myself working in the field of artifacts, in museums, or a village of living history like Williamsburg.

The other seriously daunting realization about postdoctoral university work was the "publish or perish" aspect of academia. Not relishing the idea of having to do research under such scrutiny and risk of being unpublished, I went back to my middle-school dreams. Ginger cakes came to the rescue.

What I came to understand about myself in those two years at the University of Kentucky (UK) was that I loved all kinds of history: church history, English history, Jewish history, comparative religions, rituals and liturgies, their symbols, and texts. I especially appreciated objects used by humans throughout time. I wanted to work in the museum and archives field, not academia. The very generous staff in the UK archives invited me to volunteer with them to "test my vocation" in museum studies.

MAGNETS AROUND OUR HEARTS

My supervisors in the archives kept me occupied with lots of different projects. I learned about oral history and rare books. I removed rusting metal staples and paperclips from gubernatorial papers and helped researchers with our World War I glass slides collection. My self-manicured thumbs were used to hold down the fore-edged paintings of books being filmed for a documentary, and I encountered the amazing chapbook collection. I had the privilege of assisting the hand-press printer, learning to appreciate movable type in the process. My first year of graduate school in the archives taught me more about myself than I learned in the thousands of pages of dusty histories I read, many written by dull, unimaginative men with famous names and reputations.

Fortunately for me, the director of the UK archives saw such enthusiasm in my volunteer work that he arranged for me to study at the National Archives. While his budget did not permit him to pay me, he covered the tuition for the Certification in Archival Administration program in Washington, D.C. All I had to do was arrange my own transportation and housing. (The same uncle and aunt from my Williamsburg trip had moved to Alexandria, Va. They offered me a room.) That summer between the two years of graduate school, studying across the street from the FBI building, touring various museums and archives, and becoming fully immersed in the culture of preservation confirmed my desire to continue in the field of "practical history."

The following fall, I did not return to school with the intention of pursuing the PhD because I had discovered how diverse my interests were and that there was no single topic which interested me enough to spend years of research for a dissertation. If academia might be in my future, it was probably in some other configuration. The middle-school girl's lingering desire to pursue a doctorate did not completely go away. Only decades later was it the right time and in the right field, "practical theology."

As I've said in many classrooms and presentations on discernment, I think God places magnets around our heart that pull us toward people, ideas, subjects, places, and vocations. Sometimes those magnetic pulls are triggered by sounds or tastes, like baked ginger cakes, fresh from a brick oven. Sometimes they are spontaneous, enthusiastic responses to unexpected invitations.

———————————————— ◇ ————————————————

PONDER . . .
What images, sounds, smells, or tastes do you have of the first time you knew what you were called to do? How have you changed the way you've pursued that path?

VOCATION AND GENDER

Some of my readers, especially those near my own age, will be able to articulate how career and vocational choices have grown exponentially in our lifetimes. In the 1960s and early 1970s, feminist literature increased our awareness of the way in which women had limited choices. Most of my female college classmates chose teaching, nursing, or social work. One chose law; none chose engineering.

Today, women can choose any career, without much concern about gender equity. Sadly, I've heard a few current university students dismiss the feminist movement without realizing how much they have benefitted from it. Also, they often pose career questions focused on doing, not yet addressing how it might impact their identity or sense of being. Perhaps we all need reminding that we are human beings, not human doings.

During my son Sean's kindergarten year, a new parkway was built that changed our drive to and from school. One day, he asked me about road construction. Pointing to the berms and the trenches, he asked if God had made the ditches or if men had. I told him that I thought it was a bit of both. The people who constructed the road likely saw the value of the God-made trenches and decided to make sure they had the right amount of drainage for the parkway, so they copied them.

About a mile later, having noticed that he had asked about men, I asked him if he thought women could also have built the parkway. He replied, "Sure, if they had hardhats." It was a perspective about proper training and equipment, rather than one's gender—fair point.

———————————————— ◇ ————————————————

PONDER . . .
Were you ever in a position where your desire to do something was thwarted by a boundary imposed upon you because of your gender, your race, your religion, or some other label of identity? What happened?

HUMAN BEINGS

After we had been vaccinated against Covid, I had lunch with my friend Jane. She and our friend Helen had been among the first of my Jewish friends who actively encouraged me to write this book. At lunch that day, Jane asked me whether I had ever considered being a nun. I answered that it had been a serious consideration for me from the time I was in kindergarten.

It was an extremely hot day, and our extended family was gathered for a barbeque. My grandfather Bourgeois was a champion on the pit, basting chicken with his recipe of oil, beer, and lemon juice—delicious memories!

To protect us from the sun, there were huge, shady oak and pecan trees all around, but I remember going inside our home to be near an electric fan. The smell of wet cloth diapers and slightly sour milky formula nearly overwhelmed me. To be fair to the mothers there, the formula was probably not sour; milk always smells unpleasant to me.

I clearly remember asking immediately, "What do I do when I grow up, if I don't want to have babies?" My grandmother Préjean didn't wait for Mom to answer. She said, "You can be a nun." That suited me because I thought Sister Celine was a wonderful teacher and to be like her sounded perfectly fine. From that day until I was in high school, I thought I had settled any career or vocational question that might arise. But the memory of a spontaneous reaction to unpleasant smells is not really the heart of a vocational call. There is more to it.

Jane went on to ask me why a woman might want to choose the convent instead of marriage and family. I think that it is fair to say that many people see religious vowed life as a choice *away* from marriage when in fact, I have always seen it as a choice *toward* community. For women throughout the last two millennia, convent life has offered intellectual freedom, higher education, and a form of independence from male dominance, which was not associated with married life.

Sharing resources to live simple lives, praying together, and working for the good of others is what always drew me to the idea of religious life. A true vocational call should be more than a generic idea; it must be a specific one, one you discern carefully. By the time I was in graduate school, I was no longer sure about the convent for me. I felt clearly drawn to marry Kevin. Just as clearly, we were called to have Sean, years later.

Vocational discernment within one's own tradition takes many forms. The word *vocation* means to be called and throughout my interfaith journey, I've often heard students, who consciously are practicing discernment, use the idea of being called to express their choices of major, career, partners, or sites of employment. Vocational calls are more about what we are called to be, rather than to do. To repeat myself, we are human beings, not human doings.

This identity sometimes carries with it a sense of place, of home. It was not unusual to hear students tell me that they had chosen our university because it felt like "home," as if they were called to be there. We are all called to pay attention to the magnets around our hearts, the sense of comfort or being at home. It helps us to identify our true self: who we are called to be.

PONDER . . .
Have there been times in your life when you knew you were being called to be someone or your true self rather than to do something in a job or career?

HISTORY LESSONS

Miss House was an extremely affirming teacher. When I was in her fourth- grade class, I thought I wanted to be a playwright. I wrote two or three plays, but I only remember one. It was a work of historical fiction, filled with anachronisms and more of a skit than a full play. Miss House allowed me to cast and direct three or four of my classmates in the production. The skit focused on the myth of George Washington never telling a lie. Even though I knew that Lincoln was born 10 years after Washington died, in my play, they were friends. At the crucial scene, when George was discovered, having chopped down a healthy, fruit-bearing cherry tree, he looked at his father. With the force of a fourth-grade actor, my classmate proclaimed, "I cannot tell a lie. Abe did it!"

It sounds like I easily could have begun a career in 21st century journalism, rewriting history and distorting the truth. I wonder if the current promoters of fake news and propaganda got their start in the fourth grade. It can be either entertaining or frightening to look back and to find places where we easily might have done something very different.

CANDID SELF-EVALUATION

When we are seeking our first job, we create a resume, a summary of our educational accomplishments and experiences, which is designed to sell us to a prospective employer. But we are all more than our degrees, certificates, and job experiences. We have gifts and talents that usually don't appear on resumes. As we continue to write our spiritual autobiographies, I recommend personality inventories to discover our types, our management styles, and our strenghts. If you have access to such inventories, now is a good time to review them. Think about adjectives that others use to describe you.

For some of us, there are adjectives that we find unsettling, even offensive. Why might I have been called "officious" by one boss and "efficient" by another? Discernment involves both the assessment of our faults as well as our strengths.

PONDER . . .
What are your gifts, talents, and values that contribute to your life's work?

GURU

As children, when we played school, I played the role of teacher. After visiting Williamsburg, I wanted to be a docent and an historian. (In the U.S., a *docent* is a trained guide in a museum or historic village; in some countries, it is an associate professor in higher education.) When I was in my mid-30s, I left the museum and archives field to become a counselor and history teacher, working with students in the seventh to twelfth grades. I had a glimpse of the real importance of teaching.

I was invited to a graduation party, hosted by an Indian family. There were women dressed in the most gorgeous saris in more colors than I can list. A sitar player performed while we feasted on dishes from one of the finest Indian restaurants in our region. After dinner, my student's father went to the podium and called for the distribution of gifts.

As each teacher was given a gift, the father explained the story, written in Hindi in gold letters on a black background. (Even without knowing the story, the gift was stunning.) He translated the story of a young student who was awakened from a deep sleep to find God and his *Guru* (teacher) at the foot of the bed. The young man knew he was to bow to show respect, but he couldn't figure out to whom he should bow first—God or Guru. Suddenly, God said, "Bow to Guru first, for without your Guru, you would not know me."

Years later, at a similar party, I was given a gift, referring to the same story. The message, handwritten by my student, reads, "I bow to the Guru who by the application of the collyrium of knowledge opens the eyes of one blinded by the disease of ignorance." (Collyrium is a salve which soothes the eyes.)

PONDER . . .
Without our gurus, we would not know God. Who have been your mentors who prevented the blindness of ignorance?

Gracious God,
I thank you for the teachers, mentors, and companions
who have helped me to know myself and you, more deeply.
Help me to recognize opportunities in my own life
when I may serve as a mentor to others.

4

Seven Only Children

Understanding Family Identity; Overcoming Obstacles

"Sticks and stones may break your bones,
but words will never hurt you," is a lie.

As we are journaling and remembering, beginning to compose parts of our spiritual autobiographies, we continuously confront the ultimate question of identity. The answers are many and complex because we are constantly changing and, hopefully, maturing along the way. One day, we feel like Superwoman and the next, like nobody. Another reason the answers are complex, is because we are not the only one defining ourselves. We are constantly confronting labels imposed upon us by others, sometimes traumatically.

STICKS AND STONES

Besides the story about women building roads, my son, Sean is indeed a very deep thinker who enjoyed words. When he was about four, we were turning into a neighborhood on the way to his preschool. I engaged the turn signal, made the turn, and the signal stopped. Sean remarked that he just loved "automagic things" like that. Why not? Automatic is not nearly as mystical a word, and I like his word better.

Of course, a fascination with words and with learning can easily be dispelled by bullies in school. As a middle- and upper-school counselor, I longed for some "automagic words" that I could pass along to the parents of students who were suffering from depression and anxiety, often caused by their peers who turned their own depression into abuse of anyone who appeared a bit weaker. Some of the bullies were children of abusive or absent parents, and you might imagine the horrible evenings they endured before bringing their anger into school the next day. Bullies are not born; they are formed. I knew from my own experience that they can damage our sense of worth.

A feeling of inferiority is not easy to dispel. In my seventh-grade year, a group of peers began passing notes in class. Somehow, the notes were never caught by the sisters or lay teachers. They were passed from person to person, and when I was left out of the line of recipients, I knew it was over. I knew that recess would come and that no one would speak to me. I had no idea what I had done, and no one would tell me. But it was over. Suddenly, I was no one's friend. One day, all was fine, and the next day, I was out; there was something terribly wrong with me.

Fortunately, I had a wise mother who listened when I told her what had happened. She calmly suggested that what I should do the next day was to look around the playground carefully to see if there was anyone else who sat alone on a bench. She advised, "They've done this before to others. Even if you don't know it, someone else has been left out, too. Go and sit with her."

Indeed, Mom was right. There was a new girl who was sitting alone. Her parents were older and probably couldn't understand as well as Mom did. I sat next to her and asked, "Did they send a note around about you, too?" She told me that they had, and that she had no idea what she had done. We decided that as much as it hurt, at least we were not alone. We would try to ignore them. It worked fine. But I never trusted the note-passers again. Worse, I stopped trusting myself from time to time. The voice never completely leaves, does it? "You are not good enough. You are not smart enough. You are not pretty enough. No one likes you. You don't belong."

These messages rarely completely go away, no matter how many degrees or fancy professional titles and awards you earn. You always think that someone will find out that you are not as smart as they are. Those same mean girls drove one of our least confident new teachers to tears. I remember being surprised and sad that even an adult could be so hurt by these same girls.

Over the years, I have had conversations with many students and colleagues in which I attempted to be their cheerleader. I would ask them where they thought their lack of self-confidence originated. They might begin with a story about some recent incident that they thought illustrated some truth of their incompetence. After a few more questions and stories, they often revealed that they originated in a lower- or middle-school-age situation, like mine with the seventh-grade girls.

When I invited them to consider where those bullies were now, it was often surprising. Many who had reached their height of power and popularity in high school failed to be happy or successful after.

When those sad stories are revealed, I hope that they trigger compassion. With intellectual realization, we see that we aren't the losers that they said we were, then or now, giving us a chance to be compassionate with them and with ourselves. It helps us to realize how likely their meanness stemmed from abusive home situations or other unknown wounds of the body and spirit. Hopefully, it brings us to a spiritual realization that we are all children of God and that none of us is perfect or wonderful all the time. For me, the stories bring a sense that God isn't finished with any of us yet, that we are loved for who we are and not what we have accomplished.

PONDER . . .
Have you ever felt as though you were inadequate, unworthy, or not living up to your potential? Were you able to overcome those feelings, and if so, how?

OFFICIOUS

"She is really very good at her job; she's just a bit officious." I had to look it up. I was more confused by its definition and why the museum director thought it applied to me. I had never thought of myself as efficient to the point of irritation. Such efficiency as risk management was my strength, or so I thought.

In my opinion, being a risk manager is part personality and part training. I had been elected Vice-President of Efficiency by my university sorority sisters because I was organized. My job was to work as chief of staff with the executive officers, to assure their reports were filed on time. I trained new officers in their duties, maintaining our good standing with our international headquarters. I was a top-notch, efficient risk manager.

I also was an excellent money manager. Imagine four college-aged women on a cross-country camping trip from Lake Charles, Louisiana to Banff, Canada in the middle of one of the gasoline shortages in 1970s. I controlled our budget. Without a single class in accounting, I had managed to assure there was money remaining.

Many decades later, I found out that my personality is also that of a "refiner." In one of those never-ending attempts to improve myself, I had taken a leadership course (the *DiSC Profile*) which focused on the various styles necessary for building a good team. I'm a refiner. It explained a lot about the relationship with my boss and his boss who were both "creators."

Refiners have abilities to anticipate almost everything that might go wrong with an idea, project, or activity. That means we will think of all kinds of ways to *prevent* something from going wrong. The problem is that people who are creators don't want to know what could go wrong. They think that refiners are trying to criticize or, worse, thwart their brilliant ideas. They don't realize that when a refiner anticipates problems, she helps to make success more probable.

When I list my gifts and talents, I include both *officious* and *refiner* on my list. The latter helps me to understand how I work within a team. The former helps me to be cautious about being an irritant to others, even when it still stings a bit to think of myself that way.

PONDER . . .
How have you been labeled in the past by those who have their own insecurities, who tried to drag you down with them? How have you allowed your own light to shine?

CONFRONT YOUR FEARS

Besides being labeled by an adjective we'd rather not think about, we are also invited to consider our fears. Motivational speakers sometimes suggest that the word "fear" is an acronym for "false evidence appearing real." Some of us can list our top fears without much hesitation. Sometimes we don't discover them until we are in the middle of a crisis.

For two summers, I was a counselor for the Camp Fire Girls at Camp Wi-Ta-Wentin (which means "living and playing together outdoors"). I had been invited to apply for the position by a close friend, a sorority sister whom I admired. I'd grown up camping with my family, but my friend seemed to be a fearless peer, a true trailblazer.

Paula had helped me confront my own fear of being in a natural body of water where I could not feel the bottom. She knew all about poisonous snakes and how to use a brush hook properly. We even seemed to read each other's mind a few times over the course of my first summer as a camp counselor.

One afternoon, we had a small group of girls in our large canoe; I was in the front, and she was in the back. We decided that we were going to paddle up to an island in the river and take a short hike around. Just as we approached the shore, Paula said in a calm, but extremely firm tone, "Melanie, don't move. Just paddle very gently backward. Don't move your head." There was absolutely no panic in her voice; the girls were clueless. But I knew something was wrong.

As I paddled, I looked all along the shore for a water moccasin or a copperhead, but I could not see what the danger was until we were back in the middle of the river. Then, I saw it: a hornets' nest the size of my head. If I had stood up to pull the canoe to shore, I would have been stung to death, literally. Paula saved my life.

A few weeks later, I had a chance to return the favor. We took our older campers on a road trip to Kisatchie National Forest. It's a stunning place in Louisiana, and most of our campers had never been this far from home; they'd never seen any landscape besides the prairie land and bayous of southwest Louisiana. Here there were vistas of pine-covered hills as far as you could see, with deep valleys shaded by trees on either side. The view from the top of the fire tower was breathtaking. When we decided it was time to climb down, Paula asked two of the older campers to organize a twig-collecting expedition for us to make s'mores before we started for home.

She asked me to stay and let them supervise each other for a while so we could talk. After the last girl was far enough down the ladder to be unable to hear us, Paula told me that she didn't know how she was going to make it down the ladder. I looked at her white knuckles and knew she wasn't joking. Quietly, I encouraged her as we took each step. We pretended that we were having a serious conversation (We were!) and that we needed to take it very slow to finish our discussion. We rounded up the girls and all their twigs and headed for a campsite area. No s'mores ever tasted so sweet.

PONDER . . .
What are your most challenging fears? When and where have you confronted them? How has it helped you to encourage others who seem crippled by theirs?

SEVEN ONLY CHILDREN

"How in the world did you do it?" I asked Mom. I was trying to make some simple decision about my only child. She had reared seven of us in what seemed to be an effortless parenting style. Mom married just a year after she'd completed high school, and I was born 11 months later. She laughed at my question and said, "Well, I certainly didn't read any book or articles to tell me what to do!" Of course, I had devoured every published resource and maybe it was just too much conflicting information.

Mom amazed me; I still think she was a miracle worker. When asked about having a large family, she'd brush it off with true humility. She would suggest that she really hadn't reared seven children, that the three oldest had reared the other four. There is some truth to that. I can remember lots of days when we'd be working in pairs on homework or role-playing about our future careers, dreams, and aspirations. It wasn't just the older ones teaching the younger ones.

One of my brothers was an accomplished football player. I had *no* athletic skills, but I did have a high-school gym teacher who thought that we needed to kick a football through the goal posts to earn an A in his class. I was beside myself. Mark stepped in quickly and taught me to hold, throw, and kick a football. I was determined that PE was not going to ruin my grade-point-average. (Algebra was doing a fine job of that, on its own.) I'm not sure how many afternoons we spent in our huge front yard, but he saved me; I earned the A. He was five years younger, but he was my teacher.

There was another occasion when someone complimented my parents about the seven of us. Apparently, that day we must have been very well-behaved. Dad remarked that he had little to do with it. He said that my mom had reared "seven only children." I'll never forget that day. It was a rather unusual remark, but it stayed with me because I knew it to be true. Each of us got what we needed.

If we complained about a sibling, Mom would tell us that it was "just a phase." (She knew more developmental psychology than any professor.) If one of us needed help, she'd appoint the right sibling to assist. She taught me a great deal about patience and treasuring individual gifts.

Rachell left home at 18 to move to Colorado. She had more courage than I've ever had. Renée worked in law enforcement and still exudes a confident ferocity I can admire. Andrea is vice-president of a corporation, a spiritual leader in church, and the chief organizer of siblings. Mark is a successful manager in his career and our ultimate host for huge family gatherings. Matt is a surgical nurse, our family's chief medical consultant, and a gifted homilist for his church. John is still the creator and woodworker—always "the hands" in Dad's diagram. We each seemed to receive enough attention to feel like an only child.

One of my sisters was going through a rough time and my grandmother was terrified that the "wrong crowd" was influencing her. I was called in to assist, and I remember saying that I thought my sister was smart enough to recognize what was happening and if we left her alone, we would find out she knew what she was doing. She did. I wasn't wise; I'd just learned from Mom to trust.

PONDER . . .
Were you ever treated as special by someone, even when you didn't feel so good about yourself? What life-lessons from your parents do you value most?

TRUST

Dad affirmed that parenting philosophy one early morning of my junior year of high school. We were driving in the predawn hours to meet our principal and a group of other girls who were going to Dallas for a weekend to visit a group of boys from Jesuit High who had created a faith-based service group. We wanted to create a similar group at our all-female high school, and they were going to help us with the details.

I wondered if my dad was concerned because we would be spending two nights in the homes of families we didn't know—fully chaperoned, but still. This was decades before mobile phones, so he handed me a piece of paper with a name and phone number on it. It was an acquaintance of his in Dallas. He told me that if I needed anything, I could call the man, and he'd help.

I asked if he was worried about me. He responded that he wasn't concerned; he only wanted me to have access to immediate help if the unexpected happened. Then he said, "We've taught you the difference between right and wrong. If you don't know it by now, it's our fault." Could there be any more powerful words of trust to keep me thinking right and behaving well?

FAMILY IDENTITY

My grandfather and dad were pharmacists who ran our family business. When I was in my early teens, I heard my grandmother's remarks, which instilled pride in being a Préjean. One of her friends had a grandson who was in some sort of trouble, which made the evening paper. With a "tsk, tsk" kind of sound and a measure of pity in her voice, she said, "Préjeans don't do things like that." Her message was received, loud and clear.

When some of my high-school classmates started experimenting with marijuana, I steered clear of any party or gathering that might have the substance. I was terrified of being caught unaware in a place where there might be drugs. It might destroy my family, I thought. A pharmacist connected to illegal substances, even if it occurred peripherally, seemed too perilous to risk. "Préjeans don't do things like that," and they certainly don't jeopardize the family livelihood or reputation. Fortunately, my close friends never were rebellious. We were an abstemious group. Once we were 18 (the legal drinking age), we would mix up one batch of strawberry daiquiris for six of us. We drank for taste, not effect.

My parents have gone to heaven, and we are left to pass along these traditions of parenting and pride in the family name to the next generations. After Mom died, my youngest brother asked us all if we thought we were now orphans. I think our parents still are with us in many ways. We hear their wisdom in our own voices as we make observations or tell stories and jokes. They were both amazing cooks, and we have all inherited those skills. Though we do go occasionally, we do not have to visit their graves to know that they are always with us and in their 15 grandchildren and 18 great-grandchildren, and counting.

———————————— ◇ ————————————

PONDER . . .
What family traditions do you plan to pass along to the next generation?

———————————————————————

MESSIAH COMPLEX

A healthy part of discernment and spiritual assessment is a solid focus on our strengths. There are many methods available for finding our own, but we need to keep an eye on our real strengths and purpose, not be misled.

A particular pitfall of ministry is one which allows us to forget that we work for God and not as God. When we worked together in campus ministry, Fr. Ron used to say that our job was/is to help people hear the voice of God in their own lives, "The job of preachers is to speak *about* God and not *for* God. Those who think they have the authority to speak *for* God easily slip into thinking they *are* God."

Besides leading into very unhealthy relationships with others, we can also slip into very unhealthy relationships with ourselves. We try to "save" others, forgetting that we are not the messiah. We cannot do it all.

Thomas Merton suggested this is a type of violence within our current mindset. In *Conjectures of a Guilty Bystander* he wrote, "The rush and pressure of modern life are a form, perhaps the most common form, of its innate violence. To allow oneself to be carried away by a multitude of conflicting concerns, to surrender to too many demands, to commit oneself to too many projects, to want to help everyone in everything is to succumb to violence. More than that, it is cooperation in violence" (81). I've learned that even if we don't have a messiah complex, we can still be overcome by too many requests. We need to discern carefully, to say "no," especially when we find ourselves without appropriate times of resting. Faithful Jews understand this weekly break, Sabbath—the rest our society seems to ignore it.

I hope that this chapter has given you an opportunity to explore the ways in which you have felt like either an incompetent failure or a messiah. And, I hope you have heard the invitation to discern your best response to what you are being called to be. When the violence of busyness threatens to overwhelm you, add a healthy sprinkling of three little words, "No. Thank you."

PONDER AND PRACTICE . . .
Here is one way to reduce the violence of busyness:

Begin your day with at least 10 full minutes of silence, without words to read or recite; silence, without words to type or construct; and silence, without phones to answer. Before you turn on your computer or check your voice mail, create a space for your Guardian Angel to do her job: to stand guard so you may listen as God reminds you that you are loved, that you have enough, that you do enough, that you are enough. At the end of 10 minutes, ask God to enlighten your hands as you type or write your list of things to do, assigning a priority to each item within that list.

The Light of the Now
To see again—to focus on today, the
bright gift of the present moment,
I must remove the drapes of anxiety
about the future.
I must draw back the voile,
pull the cords which open the blinds to
allow the light to illuminate each day,
revealing the world which is true,
the earth and her blessings—to invite
the light of the now to shine.
©2020 M-PS
Angel of God, my guardian dear; to whom God's love commits me here;
ever this day, be at my side; to light and guard, to rule and guide. Amen.

5

Write Your Own Script

Forming Personal Identity

Handwriting is a spiritual designing, even though it
appears by means of a material instrument.
—Euclid

Our lives are a process of creating the person we want to be. Sometimes that means we must find ways of breaking through the barriers which are preventing us from becoming our true selves. Fear, as I mentioned before, is one of those barriers. But there might be other barriers we encounter, too.

THE CHALICE

When I was in high school, we played a parlor game, likely based on Jungian archetypes. If you are so inclined, do this exercise before you read any more of this essay, describing each object with as much detail as possible.

──────────────── ◇ ────────────────

EXERCISE
Imagine yourself on a path. In very clear detail, describe it and everything along the way: an obstacle, a wooded area; a drinking vessel and what you do with it; a body of water; a wall; and what is on the other side of the wall.

──────────────────────────────────

I asked you not to read this part of the essay until you had finished the exercise because I am going to tell you what I said, explaining what the exercise is supposed to indicate, without influencing your answers. My path was an unpaved road; it had worn places of broken shell on which tires had left tread, and there was a bit of grass in the middle. (Small shells harvested from the Gulf were used to pave rural roads or driveways in southwest Louisiana, instead of pea gravel or small stones.) It was wide enough for two or three people to walk alongside each other, but there was no traffic on it. I left the road to walk into a wonderful forest, which had a few paths and lots of shady trees.

The obstacle was a large, flat-topped boulder like one we had on our playground at school. I merely walked around it. In the clearing, there was a beautiful chalice with jewels on it. I left the chalice on the boulder for others to see or have. The water was a lovely little brook, and I waded into it and across. It was nice, but I didn't spend much time in it. The wall was a castle wall, with a large door; I pushed it open and walked through. On the other side was a lovely meadow filled with yellow flowers, a castle, and more woods to explore.

What is it all supposed to mean? The path is what we think of our lives. How wide or easily traveled it is, indicates whether we think we are meant to be alone or with others. The woods are our overall impression of life, filled with green and growth or stark and foreboding. The obstacle represents all obstacles and how we handle difficulties or even crises. The drinking vessel represents our mother; the body of water represents our view of sex; the wall is our view of death. Our view of the afterlife is what we imagined on the other side of the wall.

If you participated in the exercise, imagine explanations for the answers you gave. For instance, I don't usually accept obstacles; I find ways around them. Also, I think of Mom as a lovely, jeweled chalice that is not mine to keep. It makes sense that as the first of seven children, I knew how much my siblings would need her help to navigate life.

PONDER . . .
What insights did you glean from this imaginative exercise? What obstacles have your overcome?

BEYOND CAROLINGIAN MINUSCULE

The air in our living room was fresh with the fragrance of the pine Christmas tree as I unwrapped a gift from Dad. It was curious, since most of our gifts from Mom and Dad were placed under the tree, unwrapped. This one was from Dad, only. It was a beautifully illustrated book published by National Geographic entitled, *The Age of Chivalry*. It became my most treasured possession throughout my undergrad

AN APARTMENT NEXT TO THE ANGELS

and graduate years. It is still shelved in my bookcase, so I see it almost daily.

I found the pageantry and the artisans of the Middle Ages captivating, especially the monks and nuns who so carefully copied manuscripts with elegant precision, illuminated letters, and skillfully decorated margins using their gifted imaginations. I tried my hand at calligraphy a few times. I even took a couple of classes, but I never stayed with it. I never felt adequate copying the Carolingian miniscule. Maybe I lacked the discipline to master the script through practice. Maybe it didn't feel creative enough because it demanded so much practice. Still, I wondered what it was that drew me to those medieval calligraphers.

When the *Heritage Edition of the St. John's Bible* was booked for exhibition on our campus, I arranged a meeting with a local artist and calligrapher to discuss how we might prepare our students to enhance their experience of the exhibit. I shared with her why I was so enthusiastic about this opportunity, a little about my career path toward campus ministry, and how this exhibition was reminiscent of my first career within the museum field. Toward the end of our conversation, I lamented my inability to stick with learning calligraphy, to which she confidently replied, "You don't need to copy a medieval script, someone else's script, to be a calligrapher. You can use your own hand-writing."

Her words created a paradigm shift for finding my own voice. They were an invitation to discover my artistic self, but it was so much more. It wasn't the first time I'd rejected rules, norms, or someone else's script. I had spent hours in high school creating my own handwriting, expressing my individuality apart from the Palmer method in our penmanship classes. Now I was in my 60s, and it was time for another way of revising Melanie and preparing for my retirement.

PONDER . . .
Have you ever broken free of a paradigm, someone else's formula or script?

CHANGING THE SCRIPT

There is a double meaning in the notion of changing the script. While I might have learned to use my own handwriting to create my own script, I also find that discernment is a discovery that gives us a chance to change the whole story, like the script of a play. I think there is value in both approaches.

Discernment is about discovering a sense of call. It is also about revising, asking, and answering questions over and over until you have a sense of the right ones for you. It is never settling for the "one and done" answer, like the decision we make about what to have for dinner. It's knowing we aren't finished completely because we are always growing, revising into our true selves.

In this constant revision, I have refined my personal sense of identity. I am a Catholic, but not one who believes that Christians are any more loved or saved by God than anyone else. I'm a Catholic who is delighted to be part of a local Jewish community as a learner. I am a woman and a feminist, but I have a husband and son whose perspectives I appreciate. I am straight and cis-gendered, but I have lots of LGBTQIA friends and family members whom I love. I am an American, but not the kind of exclusionary one embodied in some political propaganda. I am of Acadian ancestry, but I have been an Anglophile since I was 9. I am a retired woman who feels 40, yet I recognize that the mirror doesn't lie. I am on a mission to dispel the myth that we are disconnected, that anyone is outcast. And I say this with the conviction that my "I am" is a tiny bit of the great "I AM" of Moses' burning bush.

There is a wonderful tale from the Jewish Hasidic tradition which tells of Rabbi Zusha who was asked by his disciples why he was crying on his death bed. He had done so many *mitzvot* (good deeds) in his lifetime that his students thought he surely had a reward waiting in heaven. But Zusha said he was crying because he was afraid because he was sure God was not going to ask him "Why weren't you more like Moses or more like King David?" He was afraid that God would ask him instead, "Why weren't you more like Zusha?" He was crying because he wasn't sure what he would answer.

PONDER . . .
How might you change your script to become more like the person you know God wants you to be?

LET ME THINK

At the end of my first year of college, my parents moved our family to a home within a neighborhood. We'd grown up on land owned by my grandparents, in a part of town where we had few close neighbors with children. Suddenly, there were lots of families within an easy walk on our block.

One family had a particularly delightful little boy with a very grown-up name, George. I thought he was rather like an old soul in a boy's body. In the middle of a conversation one afternoon, it was confirmed. With our feet dangling into the cool waters of our backyard swimming pool, we engaged in a conversation about his life. Suddenly, an ambulance sped down the boulevard in front of our house. Above the din of the siren, George declared, "I think that lady is going to have a baby." I was quiet for a moment before I asked him if he thought it might be someone besides a woman on her way to the hospital, that it might be someone who'd broken a leg or something else.

George quickly looked at me and said, "Let me think!" He firmly placed his thumb and pointer finger up against the bridge of his nose as he tightly closed his eyes, remaining deeply in thought for more than a few seconds. Finally, he opened his eyes and spread his hand in delight. "Yes!" he replied, "It might be someone else on their way to the hospital."

I often think that little George's pondering posture is extremely helpful to those of us who are asking ourselves ultimate questions. What a perfect way to ignite the energy of the pause and declare aloud, "Let me think."

PONDER . . .
When was the last time you fully paused to ponder one of life's important questions?

BECOMING ATTENTIVE

In Chapter 1, I mentioned an inviting phrase from the Greek Orthodox liturgy. The priest chants, "Let us be attentive," before the readings from Scripture. I love this phrase!

It seems to be very much in line with the way in which the story of Moses unfolds. We must be attentive to all kinds of signs and wonders, memories and experiences, people, and places. It isn't unlike what I wrote earlier about the magnets around our hearts. These are all indicators of what we are meant to be considering in our discernment.

In listening to the stories of those with whom I've journeyed, one of my responses has been to repeat phrases that the storyteller uses as a way of inviting her to think deeper about what she is saying. It can be an effective way of clarification for answering important questions.

Sometimes we use metaphors repeatedly which have unexpected somatic consequences. When I've used phrases like, "hanging on by my fingernails" or feeling "stabbed in the back" or" cut off at the knees," I sometimes notice my body reacting. Symptoms develop and call me to attention about my feelings.

If we are rather dedicated to journaling, it is helpful to set aside time on a regular basis to read what we have written and to look for patterns. Every couple of weeks works best for me. If I'm using a word or phrase over and over without fully realizing it, I think of it as a burning bush. I must stop to take a closer look, to marvel at it. I might also mention it to a spiritual companion or director to see if there is some insight to be gained, which I might be missing. It needs my attention.

PONDER . . .
Review what you've written in your journal for the last few weeks or months. Did you use any term in a particular place or repeatedly, which calls for your attention?

ON ROSH HASHANAH

Clarification often happens when we gain a new perspective. I've always been one of the first to sign up for professional development opportunities, and of course, my graduate studies were part of my interest in alternative viewpoints and my thirst for knowledge. After the doctorate in ministry, I was looking for something to increase my skills in interfaith work and my knowledge about other religions.

As I wrote earlier, I applaud and highly recommend the work of the *Interfaith Youth Core* (IFYC) and its founder, Eboo Patel. When he teamed his research with Dominican University in Chicago, their interfaith leadership training was exemplary and helped me to develop new insights and skills. Even after decades of working with people of faiths other than my own, I had so much to learn about cultivating "appreciative knowledge" and the ethics of pluralism. In our ministry, IFYC helped us to develop effective initiatives: action plans with careful assessment on campus. Personally, I felt affirmed as an interfaith chaplain.

Even with enthusiastic students on board for the interfaith work and our successful activities, I had a personal desire to pursue more study. I found it with an adult Jewish learning program at a synagogue, not far from campus. Every Thursday morning for two years, I became a student with Jewish adults from across our city. At the end of the core curriculum, there was a celebration, during which I was invited to speak about my experience. In my reflection, I expressed my gratitude for feeling appreciated and affirmed, for the brilliant teachers and students who had been with me on the journey. They welcomed me as a stranger until we studied together as friends.

About a month later, the rabbi called to ask me if I would be willing to expand my brief remarks and to tie them into the message of the High Holy Days. He asked me to preach on *Rosh Hashanah*, the Jewish New Year. He explained that some of what I said he thought his whole congregation needed to hear and that sometimes we listen best when we hear from someone other than the person who usually preaches.

You may not realize it, but as a lay person I am not allowed to deliver a homily within a Catholic Mass. While not allowed to preach in my own faith tradition, I had been invited to preach in a synagogue! No words can describe that mystical experience of standing on the *bimah* before hundreds of people, helping them to understand how beloved they were, how honored I was, and how pleased I believed God was with what we were doing. It was an interspiritual experience of a lifetime.

PONDER . . .
Have you ever been invited to venture far from your comfort zone and discovered a perspective beyond your wildest imagination? Have you ever received affirmations you didn't expect?

MYSTIC PEREGRINE

A more imaginative way to gain clarification is to picture a soaring peregrine falcon, a majestic bird I first glimpsed from many meters below as I paddled through whitewater on the New River in West Virginia. Chaperoning ninth graders on such a potentially life-threatening adventure is no mean task, especially for someone who is not fond of swimming in water deeper than five feet. From the bottom of the canyon, I was seeking comfort, searching for helpful insight. When the falcon appeared several times on our trip, I began to think that she might be my *totem*, my spirit animal, as First Nation peoples would say.

I studied a bit more about these amazing birds, after my first rafting trip. They live on every continent, except Antarctica. They can soar to over 3,000 feet above ground, then fly toward their prey at over 200 miles per hour, and they are among the fastest members of the animal kingdom.

Decades after that river trip, while I was sabbatical, I visited Norwich, England. After meditating in the shrine of Julian, a place where many mystical experiences occurred to this great spiritual guide, I saw another peregrine as she hovered near the Cathedral. She dipped her wing in my direction, and I was sure her presence was providential.

Peregrine also means *pilgrim*, and as I embarked on my own spiritual pilgrimage in writing these essays, I needed to keep her in mind, my mystic peregrine. She doesn't sing sweetly like a nightingale or soothe her listeners like a mourning dove. Her call is staccato-like and persistent. She demands attention as she sings of a life on the edge, almost unsettled, but never relenting. I found writing these essays like her call: mystical, a spiritual encounter of both invitation and command.

I've always been intrigued by the stories of the great Saints and Mystics, in capital letters. Much like Merton's quote about becoming a saint (with a lowercase *s*) in my Prologue, I've discovered that there is a way to become an everyday mystic, with a lowercase *m*. It means to seek and discover the presence of the Sacred in ordinary places and people. It isn't an ecstatic experience of the supernatural, visions, or out-of-body events. It is a deliberate search and discovery of God in nature and people; in creative works of art, music, and poetry; at the moments of birth and death; in the laughter of a child and a warm breeze from the salty sea.

This chapter invites you to ask your ultimate questions about your beliefs or worldview and to revisit your journal, often. You can soar like a falcon and view life from hundreds of yards above and ask mystical questions, looking for sacred encounters and insights about meaning and purpose.

———————————— ◇ ————————————

PONDER . . .
Have you ever recalled an experience with a bird's eye view and discovered something new or transformative? Have you ever imagined yourself as an everyday mystic?

ASKING THE RIGHT QUESTIONS

In 2017, I was awarded a sabbatical with the Margaret Beaufort Institute of Theology (MBIT) in Cambridge, England. It was a "dream come true" for an Anglophile like me, an opportunity to practice discernment for myself as I approached retirement, a chance to be part of a Catholic women's institute, which happened to house the Woolf Institute for

Jewish Studies, at the time. With my family's blessing, I left home to spend nine weeks in Cambridge, to think, to pray, to ponder, and to discern.

In my heart, I knew that I had to ask many of the questions about my religion and my beliefs that I couldn't ask aloud as a minister working for a Catholic university and by extension, the Roman Catholic Church. I was in a safe place at MBIT, with women of my own faith who treasured the questions, too. There are over 100 libraries in the colleges and federations of Cambridge University, so I was in the right place to read, explore, question, and discern.

I engaged in several regular spiritual practices with the women of MBIT, and I spent hours journaling and practicing calligraphy. By walking to the market or the chaplaincy for Mass, I logged over 12,000 steps a day, providing ample time to think. Within my research time and a small bit of teaching, I asked all kinds of questions and searched for answers of connection. It was a *last career* journey of discernment, or more realistically, it became a quest to find my retirement identity. It was a way of revisioning and changing my script.

I reminded myself of the first ideas I had taught my students, to try to approach discerning without a preconceived outcome. True discernment comes with looking at all the possibilities objectively, without attempting to make things fit. It's not unlike the wonderful English detective stories which helped me through the first months of our pandemic. You must consider all the information and not look only for clues to fit the first culprit that you identify. You could be lead down the wrong road, and the innocent will suffer.

One of the byproducts of letting go of our preconceived notions is that we learn to think more about questions before we settle for answers. Most of those with whom I've worked in discernment who were the most successful, were the ones who realized that our first task is to make sure we are asking the right questions. If we go along our merry way as we are asking the wrong question, we will never truly be satisfied. Likewise, if we accept simple answers to complex questions, we will be led far astray.

PONDER . . .
Have you ever discovered that you were asking the wrong question?
How have the right questions helped you to rewrite your own story?
What questions remain in your search?

Sacred Presence
Thank you for the gift of my hands and my mind.
Guide my thoughts as I write.
Teach me to ask the right questions.
Help me to know how best
to write my own script,
with careful lines and enough flourishes
to keep life interesting.

6

Perceptions Matter

Interpreting Painful Scenarios

Do not subject me to the will of my foes, for false witnesses
and unjust accusers have appeared against me.
—Psalm 27:12

In our quest to answer life's ultimate questions, we are invited to pause periodically. We revisit our questions of personal identity and our theological answers. Each of these new visits helps us to think more clearly about how we think the world works and how we fit into it. We come to know more about ourselves as we move through the worlds of work and family, changes of career or geography, new books we read, and classes we attend.

These invite us to clarify what we think we know and believe. We address the perceptions we have and the motives of others. We look back upon past hurts and reassess those situations. Occasionally, we encounter a challenge which forces to us reconsider or change direction, completely. Sometimes it is a result of not hearing something quite correctly.

ONE BELL

One of my earliest memories is of my paternal great-grandmother's home. There were sheep and their little lambs rambling all over her yard. We entered the front door of the house directly into a long, dark parlor, or maybe it was a wide hallway. She sat, as if on a throne, at the end of the hallway with everyone sitting around her like you imagined ladies-in-waiting near a queen. It might as well have been a foreign court because they all spoke French. None of my grandparents or their siblings learned to speak English at home, and I never heard my great-grandmother speak it.

On one visit, I heard her say, "*Qui n'entend qu'une cloche n'entend qu'un son.*" (It is from Balzac and means, "One who hears only one bell, hears only one sound.") I'm reasonably sure she was using it to give advice to her listeners or maybe admonish someone she thought was gossiping, but I can also see how that quote is an expression of the way in which our culture has deteriorated. It's about hearing and listening, two distinctly different concepts, which we conflate, often.

What happens when people think they have all the news, but they only watch the fake news channel, owned by propagandists? I prefer to think I know the whole story, but I might have heard only part of it.

We know sad stories of those who label and isolate at the first lie they read in social media. Maybe we need the sounds of a bell chorus or two, more voices to be included. Maybe we need to learn to listen.

PERSPECTIVE

For me to assume the position as director of campus ministry, I needed a third graduate degree. I was excited about the idea of more study, but apprehensive about the closest Catholic school of theology because I'd heard some negative stories about how women were treated there.

Fr. Ron was a graduate of St. Meinrad and reminded me that I should make my own decision, not to rely on what others said. He was so right. I loved my time there and all I learned from the monks and lay professors. Fr. Damian "Damo" introduced us to the writings of feminist scripture scholars and in person, to two of them at an annual conference of the Society of Biblical Literature. Professor Jefford taught us to differentiate between what a passage says and what we've been taught to think it means. He even enlisted my support in trying to help a classmate who couldn't imagine that she was to read and only summarize without *explaining* what it meant. It was frustrating.

PONDER . . .
Have you ever realized that you were looking at something from only one viewpoint? Was it an opinion you were taught, rather than your own?

MISUNDERSTOOD

Some misunderstandings take us by complete surprise. In Chapter 1, I relayed the notion that theologians insert their own theology into their work and how we discover it in their writing. I also learned to be cautious about taking too human an approach to the study of theology. In essence, I wrote in my notes, that we need to remember that God is God, and we are not.

Because we are human, our descriptions of God have limits, boundaries. God exists beyond anything we can imagine. When we try to make God in our own image, to speak for God or think we have all the answers, it creates walls which limit God; it puts God in a box. "That," one of my first graduate professors told us, "is *idolatry*." This idea has invited me on countless occasions in the past 20 years to explain how I try to keep expanding rather than limiting my understanding of God. But language is a tricky thing, and understanding is not always easy.

In 2019, I attended a retreat with the Sisters of St. Benedict in Ferdinand, Indiana. It was a retreat about images of God, and we were encouraged to be very creative in our responses to the scripture passages. I loved the expansiveness of the messages and shared the story above, quoting that final line about idolatry. Sr. Karen asked for me to explain what I meant when I said that God was like the Dollar Tree. I couldn't figure out what she meant until I realized that when I'd said, "idolatry," she had heard "a Dollar Tree," a national chain of discount stores with bright yellow bags. My images of God as an idol in a box became an idol in a yellow bag.

PONDER . . .
When was the last time you were misunderstood or misquoted? How did you reconcile what you said with what was heard? Did it make you a better listener?

VERTIGO

As if fear of a pandemic wasn't bad enough, I awoke one morning before dawn and the room was spinning, wildly. It didn't stop spinning for over 12 hours as I lay as still as possible on the bed. I couldn't walk one step without a profound fear of falling. This was vertigo, and I now know that my inner ear crystals were wreaking havoc on my body.

A few weeks later, I found a remarkable reference to my experience in a study course on *Devarim* (Deuteronomy) with my Jewish friend and mentor, Deborah. She introduced us to Chapter 32, in which Moses recites a poem to the gathering of Israel. The English, "Give ear. . ." is in Hebrew, *ha'azinu*. The Hebrew is also translated as "Listen with the ear." The Hebrew word for balance, *izun* has the same root letters as *ha'azinu.* Ancient Hebrew connected the ear/listening and balance, long before medical science helped me understand my vertigo.

This little language lesson did more than connect balance to listening, it helped me to see that for us to have a balanced view of anything, we need to listen, closely. We are invited to "listen. . . with the ear of your heart," as St. Benedict writes in his *Rule* (Chittister, 19). We also must listen to multiple voices to gain perspective, not just to understand theirs, but to understand our own better. Listening matters.

PERCEPTION IS REALITY

In the non-profit and education positions I've held, there have been significant development or fund-raising components. For a capital campaign at the independent school, outside consultants conducted a survey of various constituents to determine the feasibility of different approaches to a proposed campaign. I remember that we were told continuously, "Perception is reality." In other words, it doesn't matter what you do or how well you do it, it is what potential donors *think* you do that will determine what they are willing to contribute to any proposal.

Another quote I try to remember is, "They will soon forget what you said, but they will never forget how you made them feel." Feelings and perceptions intertwine. My most painful memories are of being misunderstood or worse, deliberately misquoted.

EGO WOUNDS

In Chapter 8, you will read my story of the child-birthing method we studied for our first and only child. It taught me to focus on the labor and not to try to distract myself from the hard work of giving birth. Another very important life-lesson in that class was the explanation of the postpartum healing process. The uterus expands to hold more than a dozen pounds of baby and fluid. When the placenta detaches, it leaves a very large open wound, larger than the size of your open hand. As the uterus returns to its pre-pregnancy size (a tightly folded fist), the wound decreases in size. As the wound becomes much smaller, faster healing is facilitated.

As we move days, months, or years away from the initial wounds of broken relationships, with the connecting pain and anger, it is important that we try to reduce the wounds. Sometimes, it's ego that must be reduced, so that the wound will be allowed to decrease and heal properly. I am sure I will never completely forget some actions, but I do try to make conscious efforts to try to forgive persons.

One way to do so is to look for the wounds in others, to try to understand them or their misguidedness. As a Catholic, I picture the crucifix and recite the quotation from Jesus, when he asks God to, "forgive them; for they do not know what they are doing" (Luke 23: 34).

PONDER . . .
When have you been able to reduce the size of an ego wound? Have you ever helped others experience such healing?

MOTIVE MATTERS

Besides linguistic and perception issues, some misunderstandings are a result of our assumption of motive. For example, two completely different responses can result from the same action, depending upon our interpretation of motive. Suppose I walked across campus and came upon a group of students I knew well. If I slapped one on the shoulder and said, "Hey! What's going on?" he would have responded with a laugh and told me they were planning what they were going to do after the recital on Friday.

Alternately, if I walked across campus and encountered a different group and mistook someone who looked like, but was *not* that same student, and I did the same thing, what would happen? If the group had been planning something far less appropriate on Friday night, they would not have reacted with the same jovial response as those in the first scenario. They might have perceived that my motive was to catch them and punish them. It would be the same jolly slap on the back and the same question, but quite a different response. Our perception of motive matters.

PONDER . . .
Where have you been able to get beyond initial feelings to find the real motive or to reconcile with someone who hurt you?

SAY AND MEAN

I mentioned Professor Jefford above; here is a more detailed explanation for what happened. After we read a particular passage to ourselves, he asked the class what it said. One woman kept replying, "I think that the writer means. . ." He stopped her and repeated that he wasn't asking for meaning, just for the facts. He had to repeat himself several times. It was exasperating to all of us when she could not seem to grasp that we were not being asked to interpret, but simply to state *what* the author said.

We were encouraged to use different versions (Greek, Latin, Hebrew, or other English translations), but we had to focus on what was said and attempt to completely remove our preconceived notions of what we thought the passage meant. Preconceived notions are very difficult to leave aside.

Language is powerful and the study of it is fascinating. I learned to take a closer look at the text, to eliminate the extraneous and the interpretations of others. I began to read gospel passages more closely and realized how often the writers had inserted a commentary, which had nothing to do with what Jesus was supposed to have said.

For instance, few Christians realize how often the gospel writers' interpretations of the motives of the Pharisees are intertwined with the text of a story. It happens so often that we fail to see that it is commentary, which might be biased, and not the story at all. That's when we might start to question motive, or at least I do.

"HEBREW SUNDAES"

As in my example about listening and balance above, sometimes the roots or original meanings of words are filled with important spiritual lessons. We lose those connections when we rely only on one English translation or what others tell us the text means for us today.

After I finished my doctorate in ministry, I enrolled in a Hebrew class on Sunday mornings at a local synagogue. With every new word we learned, we began with our assessment of the root letters (usually three consonants) and their many meanings. When I realized how many words can come from three letters, it was both amazing and deeply spiritual. It pointed to the deeper interconnectedness of things, which are not so obviously interconnected on the surface.

Consider this idea with English consonants. "HS" can mean house or hose. And hose can mean either stockings (which women rarely wear anymore) or a device for delivering water from the faucet to the roses you are watering or the car you are washing. "BBL" can be bible, babble, or bubble, the latter of which can mean either something created from glycerin or chewing gum, or our Covid definition of a group of people who consistently meet in safety during a pandemic. The possibilities can let our imaginations soar.

I won't belabor specifics or attempt to offer lessons in Hebrew, but those classes became such a treat that I started thinking of them as "Hebrew sundaes." Studying scripture from the Jewish perspective became an adventure and I began to see how Jewish commentators noticed the letters and used their arrangement within a word to reveal something about the arrangement of the words within the text.

The Torah was like a mysterious spiritual puzzle, revered and treasured. It also became clear to me how open the text can be to interpretation and re-interpretation. You can read a text every year, and it means something different each time because you've changed. I guess that's why it's called the "living word of God." Yet multiple interpretations caused serious problems in Christian history.

The Protestant Reformers of the 16th century each chose one or two verses upon which to base their new church communities. One interpreted predestination as the ultimate answer, while another saw the modern world as threat. One verse seemed to forbid the use of air for inflating tires while another forbade women from wearing jewelry or make-up. All these different interpretations, which led to more and more fracturing of the Christian church, caused the Catholic hierarchy to decide that it was dangerous to allow untrained people to read the Bible in the vernacular. In the 1960s, when I was a child, we were told what the Bible meant. I hardly imagined that in my adulthood, I would be allowed to read it on my own.

Whether we are thinking about "idolatry in yellow bags" or about "Hebrew sundaes," the way we read and listen so that we might interpret and internalize religious concepts is part of what forms each of us in our spiritual development. If someone says something that I find unsettling, it is necessary for me to clarify, "Did you really mean that?" I also think of it in my interfaith work.

Namaste was the greeting we used in India. It means, "The God within me greets the God within you." It's a perfect word for acknowledging that I am not only greeting you as another person, but that I am greeting you as an embodiment or child of God.

That last phrase is an interesting one because it conveys a double meaning. When I say that I greet you *as* a child of God, do I mean that I think *I* am a child of God who is greeting you, or that I greet you because *you* are a child of God? Both; it means both.

In monasteries that follow the *Rule of St. Benedict*, you will frequently hear or read, "All guests are treated as Christ." Does that mean that all guests are treated as if *they* are Christ or that all guests are treated as we think *Christ* would treat them? Both; I think it means both.

When I work with people of other faiths, I attempt to see the God which they believe exists. I attempt to understand how they are listening or ignoring that God and to ascertain if I can be a helpful witness to what they are saying and not saying about that God. It's never an easy task, but it's a journey of discovery, which I find rewarding.

PONDER . . .
Are there any passages of your scripture or teachings from your tradition which you find painful? Have you found another way to read or understand the passages?

FALSE NEGATIVE

In 2020 and in 2021, I had chills and lethargy over several days with no fever. The symptoms were not acute, but I still decided to be tested for Covid. Both tests were negative. While I was very relieved not to have exposed others to the virus, the fine print of the information sheet from both tests indicated that I might have a "false negative." It strikes me that we often find ourselves in situations where we are misreading a person or situation. Perhaps, you are like I am, and you've found yourself in a situation where you read something as other than what it was and got a false negative. It's helpful to think of the acronym, Q-tip: "Quit taking it personally."

I close this chapter with one more quote: this one from my maternal grandmother. She reminded us that, "God gave us two ears and one mouth." We should listen twice as much as we talk. The following lines are part of a prayer first attributed to St. Francis of Assisi in a French publication, *La Clochette*, in December 1912. (Notice that the title of that publication is "Little Bell" or *cloche* as in the Balzac quote from my great-grandmother at the beginning of this chapter.) Understanding matters.

Lord, make me an instrument of your peace,
where there is hatred, let me sow love . . .

O Master, grant that I may never seek
so much to be consoled as to console,
to be understood as to understand.

7

A Good Cannibal

Engaging Interfaith Questions

How good and wonderful, when sisters and brothers live as one,
sharing God's love with one another, sharing that
love with everyone. . . Here God proclaims, "Life forevermore."
—*Psalm 133*, lyrics by Chip Andrus.

Faith or Works—that's a debate which Christians argue about, a lot. Within the interspiritual community, it is not such an issue; spirituality is about connection to the Divine and not about comparative soteriological theology or who will be "saved." In the communities that teach what you believe determines your fate in the afterlife, it is huge. From what paradigm are you operating?

After I left the museum field, my next career required a second graduate degree in educational psychology. In the first course, we used the word, "paradigm" repeatedly. It was the first time I had paid much attention to it, but I fully embraced the concept of a "paradigm shift." It seemed to be very relevant in my life story: finding places where I had veered from a course and moved closer to my true self.

CANNIBALS IN HEAVEN

It was a warm afternoon in the third-grade classroom of Sr. Mary Anne. There was the distant hum of the ever-present fan, but in the heat of southwest Louisiana, she must have found it unbearable in her habit with layers of black wool serge and a severely starched wimple that was designed for women in 18th-century France. Yet Sr. Anne never showed discomfort or impatience, at least never that I can recall. In fact, her patience with my life-altering question that day is a highlight of my life.

Sr. Anne was teaching us about our Catholic religion, addressing the topic of our individual salvation. In first and second grade, we had been shown drawings of a soul on the chalkboard, with a huge mark on it to

63

represent "original sin", wiped away by our Baptism, and smaller marks that were erased by our participation in the sacrament of Penance (now called Reconciliation).

In third grade, we were learning about the more abstract concept of ultimate redemption. We knew that our *Baltimore Catechism* taught that we were saved because we were Catholic—through our participation in the sacraments and our adherence to the Church's commandments. It was clear enough in print, but I was not convinced.

I raised my hand impulsively, before completely formulating my question. (I rarely found it easy to wait for a teacher to call upon me; I was the impatient eldest of seven who thought she had to blurt out what she wanted to say, or she might forget.) Sr. Anne called on me. With all the seriousness and conviction of an 8-year-old, I asked, "Sister, what if you are a cannibal on a desert island, and you've never heard of Jesus? Do you mean to say that God will not let you into heaven when you die?"

Having read about cannibals in my grandfather's *National Geographic*, I thought they were the most exotic humans I could imagine, the farthest removed from anyone I had ever known, so it made sense to me to create this hyperbolic question. Sr. Anne paused for some time to consider my question, probably took a very deep breath, then very patiently responded, "Melanie, it just *might* be possible for a good cannibal to get to heaven faster than a bad Catholic."

And there it was, and there it remains. My theology of salvation and redemption aligned with what Sr. Anne speculated, that God calls us to learn our faith in our families, and that if we live good lives in line with our traditions and God's laws, we are going to be invited to heaven. The good cannibal and I had the same statistical chance of salvation.

Can you imagine, my dear reader, how strange it is that a little Cajun Catholic, one with no acquaintances outside of that faith tradition, experienced this gentle response to her first serious theological challenge about interfaith salvation? It was the first step toward my long journey into advocacy for interfaith work. And it was my experience of this kind of tolerance and open-mindedness on the part of many other Sisters who taught me, who helped to plant my feet firmly on the path toward interfaith work.

PONDER . . .
How are teachings about salvation part of your thinking? How have they formed your image of or created your relationship with a Sacred Presence?

RELIGION CLASS AND BEYOND

Sister Cyprian was a courageous religion teacher. In high school, to learn about social justice and personal responsibility, we watched documentaries about the liberation of the concentration camps. In the 1960s, it was unusual for Catholic high school students to spend time in religion class studying the *Shoah* (Hebrew for catastrophe; the more frequently used word "holocaust" is an incorrect term because it refers to an offering which is destroyed, entirely.) We studied it as part of moral theology, rather than history. We discussed the role of good people who did nothing, including members of the Catholic hierarchy. I was outraged and fascinated by the role our own misinterpreted, misquoted Scriptures had played in persecuting the Jews throughout the ages.

Over the next months, I read every history book on Jewish-Catholic encounters, including the Crusades and the Inquisition. I encountered my first crisis of faith that year; I was embarrassed to be a Catholic.

Three years later, Sr. Martha invited me to be our school representative on the youth council for our city's National Conference of Christians and Jews. It was my first experience of interfaith conversation. Our first meeting included representatives from all the religions in our small city; I met my first Jewish, Hindu, and Muslim friends at the annual meeting. In the summer between high school and college, I read *The Source* by James Michener and met with our local rabbi for more reading about Judaism and Israel.

At university, I majored in history and researched Jewish history. I was active in Catholic campus ministry, but I never stopped feeling disturbed by anti-Semitism in my church's past. In graduate school, I majored in English history, but all my papers contained elements of Jewish history—in the Middle Ages, Renaissance, Reformation, Enlightenment, and Modern Europe. The more I researched, the more I wanted to learn.

In graduate school, I met many people who had left one religious tradition for another. I became close friends with converts of many faiths and loved listening to their stories. I asked myself many times, "Was I Catholic because I'd been brought up to be one? If I had to choose my own religion today, which one would I choose?"

Those very questions still occurred to me every semester of my tenure in campus ministry, listening to students as they told me their stories. There were angry students who had grown up in churches filled with hatred for their gender identities or sexual orientations. There were sad students whose parents had left their churches after a divorce or second marriage. There were intellectually curious students who discovered the theologies of a new religion that made more sense to them than the faith of their family of origin.

PONDER . . .
Do you have friends from other faith/religious traditions with whom you've discussed ultimate questions of life and the afterlife? How have your answers been similar? How have they been different?

FAITH AND RHETORICAL QUESTIONS

Along my interfaith path toward religious pluralism and away from exclusivism or inclusivism, I've been assisted by theologians dedicated to the task. Alan Race has inspiring and practical books about interfaith work. In the first one, he introduced these three perspectives or "isms." He has also written about his path as a Christian toward pluralism.

A compelling quote from Thomas Merton also serves as a guide for me, "If I affirm myself as a Catholic merely by denying all that is Muslim, Jewish, Protestant, Hindu, Buddhist, etc., in the end I will find that there is not much left for me to affirm as a Catholic: and certainly no breath of the Spirit with which to affirm it" (*Conjectures*, 128–29).

Besides the three perspectives defined by Race and religious tenets explored by Merton, I have encountered the challenge of defining the word "faith" (from Old Saxon, meaning "to care or hold dear; to desire; to love"). A "creed," (from Latin, meaning "I believe") is a statement of faith, often made in public. Such declarations are not a part of either Judaism or of many non-Western religions. Thus, to call their religions, "faiths" is not accurate. This leads me to rhetorical questions, ones for which I have no conclusions to offer.

Is faith a gift only given to some or is it really a wish that what we want to believe is true? Do I believe in a God who watches over me with love or do I wish for that protective companion? Is it like the security of an imaginary friend or is it real because I want it to be real? Do we gravitate toward certain religions because their teachings match the ones we already have? Or do parents and religious teachers shape our theology?

Do people who are fundamentalist in their faith really believe in a judgmental God with a tiny heaven? Is their God stingy or is heaven huge? And, if they proselytize or force their beliefs on many others, do they think it will guarantee that they are right? Is being right more important than the truth?

What is "truth," and can I ever really know it? Why do some people think they have the truth, and you have no right to question their definition?

◇

PONDER . . .

What are your rhetorical questions, ones you don't expect others to answer for you?

INTERFAITH IMAGES

As I moved along the path toward my personal interfaith theology, I began to ask more questions about the images we have of God and the way God seems to work in the world.

Remembering the theology exercise in the first chapter, our poor confused Martian wonders why we cannot accept the pantheon of Hindu traditions as easily as a Christian Trinitarian theology. How different are those nouns and metaphors from naming the God who removes obstacles, Ganesh, or the God who destroys evil, Shiva? Is Brahma also our Creator God, as well as Allah, Adonai, and the Great Spirit? Are Vishnu and Krishna human incarnations, which are very different from Jesus? Are not all these theological constructs interesting and capable of some comparison? Why must they be exclusive?

PLEASE NOTE that I am *not* saying that all religions are the same or that Buddha and Jesus are the same or anything remotely unsubstantiated, controversial, or heretical. What I am wondering is why not accept that God is unknowable, that any attempt to construct a theology is fraught with inadequacy. Instead of thinking someone has the truth and everyone else is wrong, why can't we think that maybe we are *all* wrong, because *none* of us can know God completely?

◇

PONDER . . .

Have you ever found an answer to your questions from outside your chosen faith/religion/tradition which made more sense to you about why we are here on this earth now, what we are called to be, and what will happen to us when we die?

If any of my questions above caused you discomfort, hold on. I'm not going to go all philosophical and start probing the question of whether we can ever really know anything at all or be convinced intellectually of any answers to our ultimate questions. But I do want to introduce a stand from which we can approach the questions more deeply.

Besides the introduction to feminist scripture scholars and theologians, Fr. Damo introduced us to the hermeneutic of suspicion. A hermeneutic is a perspective from which one studies or interprets sacred texts. The hermeneutic of suspicion operates from the notion that texts may not always mean what they seem to mean. This takes us back to Chapter 6 and the student who wanted to tell us what a passage meant rather than what it said. It also connects to the importance of knowing the original language of a scripture passage before you can begin to think you know the meaning.

I recommend this approach as we move to the next few chapters and toward the deeper questions of the meaning of life, into more difficult and unsettling aspects of searching for answers, which seem to elude us. If we allow ourselves to think of everything we encounter about theology, religion, or scripture with this hermeneutic of suspicion, it can be extremely freeing.

For example, imagine how nice it would be to have an alternative to the quote in Luke's Gospel, "to those who have, more will be given; and from those who do not have, even what they seem to have will be taken away" (Luke 8:18). Most of us 21st- century Americans think the passage must be about things, commodities, material possessions. What if it doesn't mean that at all?

What if it means that those who live in gratitude for the important things (love, care, justice, hope) will be given even more? But if they spend their time complaining and whining that life isn't fair and "those other people" have more stuff, then nothing is ever going to satisfy them. In other words, they will *think* they have nothing because it's been taken away, but in fact, they are looking/focusing on the wrong things.

PONDER . . .
Have you ever encountered a religious passage or teaching that did not agree with your personal theology? What did you do with this tension? Does a hermeneutic of suspicion help you to see alternative meanings?

SPIRITUALITY

It isn't unusual to have doubts about the religion you've inherited from your parents. In fact, many great spiritual masters suggest that doubts are an essential part of growth. If we merely accept all we've been taught without question, we'll never truly embrace our faith or make it our own.

Belief and faith are essential parts of my inherited religion, but actions and good deeds, *mitzvot* are essential to Judaism. What you believe doesn't matter as much as how you behave or live your life, according to one of my teachers. That resonates with me in unexpected ways. From my story of the cannibal in third grade, it's obvious that I never thought what you believed would matter to God as much as how you lived.

In addition to good works, spirituality matters more to me than creeds. My use of the word "mystic" in my essay in Chapter 5 about the peregrine points to that. I'm much more interested in connecting to the Divine Presence in life than I am in reciting doctrine. Even in reading the gospels, I have always been more interested in the spiritual teachings of Jesus, than the commentaries within the text. (I am particularly disturbed by passages assigning treacherous motives to the Pharisees, rather than merely providing a narrative of what happened or was said.)

This is where comparative spirituality is interesting. Rabbi Lawrence Kushner helped put it in perspective, when he wrote, "Spirituality is religion experienced intimately. . . where you and God meet" (*Spirituality*, 9). The word "spirituality" is of Greek origin and it "implies a split between the material world and the realm of the spirit" (10).

This duality is an intrinsic part of the teachings of Plato that we've inherited. We often see things as either/or and consequently assign superiority to one or another. Think about it: male/female; heaven/earth; spirit/matter; body/soul; Democrat/Republican, etc. For me, this creates an unnecessary tension, a discomfort in many aspects of my life.

Kushner explained that classical Hebrew makes no such distinction, "For Jewish spirituality, there is only one world that is simultaneously material and spiritual" (Kushner, *Spirituality*, 10). I have found this very helpful in expanding my understanding of how official teachings about the nature and purpose of Jesus were interpreted by the Greek thinkers. In essence, they failed to convey the Jewish spirituality of Jesus. Their trajectory of interpretations led to exceptionalism and I've doubted that since I was 8 years old. (Exceptionalism means being different, but its use implies being superior.)

Kushner's connections remind me of the work of Franciscan Friar Richard Rohr, especially in his book, *The Universal Christ*. Rohr has taken much of our either/or thinking in Christianity and been able to show the connectedness of all things, the presence of God in all of creation. His book is about spirituality more than doctrine.

PONDER . . .
Have you found conversations about spirituality more comfortable than conversations about scriptural interpretation or doctrines? If so, how have they helped you to deepen your sense of your spiritual identity?

HEAD-HEART-HANDS

Interfaith encounters occur at different levels. There are professionals in religion and theology, ministers and academics who analyze, compare, and contrast each other's doctrines, dogmas, etc. They come from two different perspectives, some aim at objective study and some want to proselytize, prove, and persuade. You might call this the "head group" because it is analytical or intellectual.

Another level of interfaith work is focused on the experiences of the other. They want to hear each other's stories, to create empathic avenues for understanding and appreciating. They might also aim to share an experience or religious ritual. We might call this the "heart group."

One type of heart experience which I've encountered was my participation in *Iftar*, the breaking of the fast at sunset during Islam's holy month of Ramadan. My first one was in a private home for about 35 people. At the first public one I attended, there were about 100 people; at the last one (pre-Covid), there were over 500. There were people from all walks of life, various ethnicities, different economic statuses, and especially an amazing variety from the different denominations or branches of Christianity, Judaism, and Islam, as well as friends who were Hindu, Baha'i, and Buddhist.

I'm usually a "head person." Studying the history and sacred texts of other religions has always captivated me. But, as I've aged, I've come to appreciate the rituals much more. I'm very attracted to experiences of prayer, worship, and spirituality. I find chants and prayers in Hebrew transcendent. The *Siddur* (prayerbook), with which I'm most familiar is used by Conservative Jews. Besides morning and evening *Shabbat* prayers, it includes commentary on those prayers, poems, and reflections, which add to and deepen the prayer experience for me.

A third type of interfaith work which attracts many of our young adults is the work of service or the "hands group." Interfaith friendships are formed from standing side-by-side, painting a fence, or planting a garden for a house you've built with Habitat for Humanity or serving lunch to 500 homeless people at the Franciscan Kitchen. When we see how people live their faith through service, we learn about their faith without ever hearing a single quote from their holy writ.

The IFYC's earliest campus chapters were called, "Better Together." Our campus formed such a chapter, which met periodically to perform service in the city, to visit houses of worship across our county, and to gather afterwards to share stories about these interreligious encounters. One afternoon, after a physically challenging day of service, one of our Hindu students remarked that she wished everyone could witness how much "better we really are together."

PONDER . . .

Have you ever noticed the eyes and smile of a friend of another faith when you were working together for some good cause or maybe when you were in prayer together during a holy day or prayer service for peace?

"HOLY ENVY"

One of my closest friends and advisors suggested that my interfaith work might be summed up in the quote from F. Scott Fitzgerald in *The Crack Up*, "The test of a first-rate intelligence is the ability to hold two opposed ideas in mind at the same time and still retain the ability to function." I'll take the notion of my intelligence from my friend as a compliment, but I really want to affirm the end of the quote, the "ability to function." I have come to think of myself as functioning at a much higher level whenever I have had a religious experience with someone of another faith, like praying together with Deborah on *Yom Kippur*, or with Cynthia at the Baha'i house, or with Haleh at the Mosque.

I have what Barbara Brown Taylor writes of so eloquently in her book, *Holy Envy*. Her stories are about teaching world religions. The book title is based upon a term first used by Church of Sweden Bishop Krister Stendahl at a press conference in 1985. You experience it when you discover something in another faith tradition that you wish you had in your own. In studying other faiths, he suggested that you leave room for "holy envy."

My interfaith experiences have been important to me. They've taught me, changed me, and allowed me to witness spiritual growth in my students. Both experiences—those that are unique to our respective traditions and those that are similar—give us food for thought and connection. They are all part of helping each other find meaning and purpose, welcoming even "the good cannibal" to our table.

PONDER . . .
Have you ever experienced holy envy?

God of All People
Help us to know you through your followers,
To learn to appreciate the diversity of your perspective,
To love all you have created,
Unconditionally.

Here are portions of the prayer I wrote for our campus on September 11, 2001. It might equally apply to our experiences of the attacks of Covid:

Loving God, we call you by many names: God, Allah, Adonai, Jesus,
Brahma, Krishna, Great and Holy Spirit, Mother Wisdom. By these
and all the names we hold in our hearts, we call upon you.

We ask you to remind us that one name above all others is you: Love.
And we ask for your presence—your embrace upon us today. We ask you
to bring us your calm, that we may avoid panic and terror, that we not
give into the fear that clouds our thinking and our speech.

We ask you to keep our minds open to each other. We ask you to give us
restraint that we not engage in speculation and accusations. Send blessings
upon the media that they will report accurately. Protect us as we move
beyond today, knowing that life will never be exactly the same again.
In your name, the God who loves us, we pray. Amen.

8
Unknown Perspectives

Reframing Memories; Welcoming the Unknown

*The unknown encompasses and permeates our lives. Whether we
are aware of it or not, it sustains and gives us life.*
—Estelle Frankel (*Wisdom*, 202)

In the process of creating our spiritual legacies, we might notice what
one of my students called "God-sequences." We notice them when
we have what we think is a new idea, but find it referenced unexpectedly
by someone else. We notice it in repetition and attribute it to
coincidence. I think they are more than random events. For example,
when I first walked through the lanes on my 2017 sabbatical in
Cambridge, I noticed them repeatedly.

Only three months after Mom died, her favorite flower decorated
the baptismal font in a tiny medieval church that I visited on my first
day. As I sat in the side chapel, I prayed for Mom, and to reduce my
anxiety about the politics in America. As I was leaving, I noticed the
Washington coat of arms on the side wall. This had been the church
of our first president's uncle. It felt as if heaven was watching over my
concerns; my anxiety was reduced. A week later, I randomly picked up
a book in the library by an author I had not known. On my walk home,
there was a flyer advertising a talk by the same author.

Similar God-sequences happened to me through an unexpected
invitation to study in Israel two years later. In the amphitheater of
Hebrew University at Mt. Scopus, I looked toward Jerusalem and
imagined biblical stories coming to life before me. Our instructor
included me on this Jewish study trip by inviting me to lead morning
meditations and to teach a couple of times, from my Catholic tradition.
Multiple perspectives help. Noticing God-sequences helps, but
sometimes we just can't know all we think we want to know.

If I encounter a story or an idea more than a couple of times over a short period of time, I assume God (or the universe) is trying to get my attention. Recently, I encountered a story in three different places, a story of two little fish who were swimming in one direction, when they encountered an older fish coming toward them. As the older one swam past, he said, "Hey, guys! How's the water?" One of the little fish said to his friend, "What's water?"

Estelle Frankel includes this story in her book *The Wisdom of Not Knowing*. She concludes with her observation that we are like the little fish; sometimes we don't "notice the very things in our lives that are most obvious and ubiquitous" (Frankel, 202). She compares the water to the unknown and ends with the quote, beneath the title of this chapter.

As we near the end of my ethical will or spiritual legacy, I want to share some ideas for handling issues without adequate answers: *Why do bad things happen to good people? Why do evil people seem to thrive, while good people seem to die early or suffer terribly? Is there anything after this life, like a heaven or a hell? Why do I stay in a church which causes me so much frustration?*

My college friend Paula was famous for saying, "There is only one thing in life of which you can be sure: *You'll never know.*" It seemed like a funny, pithy little saying at the time, but lately, I've begun to view it as an excellent life philosophy. If we can accept that there are some questions in life that cannot be answered, we might be able to reduce our anxiety levels, considerably.

THE QUESTION OF WHY

Have you ever been engaged in a serious conversation with a three-year-old who asked you what seemed a simple question, but she kept repeating after each of your answers, "Why?" I know it's happened to me dozens of times, and it began to feel like a skit with the Three Stooges—as though it wouldn't end.

Finally, I realized I could stop the "why cycle" by admitting that I really didn't know. With that came more than a little joy. By admitting I didn't know everything, climbing down from the adult pedestal, I was one with that little child, ready to sit in wonder at a universe beyond our comprehension.

Sometimes I think that the story of the Tree of Knowledge of Good and Evil in Genesis is not unlike the why cycle. We are usually taught that the story is about disobedience, and that if our original parents had been obedient, we wouldn't be having the problems we have today: crimes, death, war, etc. In other words, Adam and Eve are the reason we have Covid-19. Sorry, but I don't believe in simplistic answers, especially when assigning blame.

I think we've completely missed the message if we blame Eve and all women for sin or blame Adam for not protecting Eve. Maybe the metaphors in the story are not about evil snakes or fruits of disobedience, but about the quest to know everything. We can't. We are not meant to know everything. It's not within our capacity; there are human limitations that we must accept. Let God be God because we are not.

I am not suggesting that it is easy to accept our limits. We don't like difficult things, which is possibly why some preachers use a simplistic explanation. It is easier to perpetuate thousands of years of the subjugating and belittling of women than to think outside the box. As one of my favorite students used to say after hearing such a sermon, "Sorry, but I find that re-damn-diculous!"

Our quest to know everything is a bit like the story of hunters who set-up monkey traps by placing nuts inside of a jar. When a monkey reaches in to grabs lots of nuts, his fist becomes too large for the jar's neck. Like the monkey, we need to "let go" of trying to know everything.

When the Covid pandemic began, our world seemed to turn upside down. Fear spread as quickly as the virus; we sheltered in place and wondered about the future. We collectively and individually participated in a time of isolation, trying to stay safely involved in "flattening the curve" of the spreading menace, giving hospitals and health care workers a chance to cope effectively. We fully entered a time of *not knowing*, of having no idea when we might know much at all.

PONDER . . .
How do you cope with not-knowing? Does it cause you fear and anxiety? Has it ever brought you a freedom to imagine, to dream, to wonder?

REFRAMING

When we were pregnant with Sean, there were two distinctively different methods of preparing for birth. The more well-known used the concept of distraction to alleviate the *pain* of the contractions. It involved a multi-syllabic chant with shallow breathing and encouraged the mother to focus on an object or place in the room, away from her body.

An alternative method, the one which we chose to study, did the reverse. Instead of short rapid breathing, we practiced breathing in very deeply and exhaling slowly. (In Yoga, it is a "cleansing breath.") We were taught to pay close attention to each contraction, to be attentive to its rhythm and intensity—using the metaphor of an ocean wave, which reaches its peak and then descends, flowing onto the shore. The birth partner used a monitor or a watch to act as coach or narrator, helping the mother with information about each crescendo, assisting in awareness of the tremendous work, the labor in which she was engaged.

The method we used involved one of my favorite psychological terms, "reframing." Labor was not punishment for Eve's disobedience nor was it the *pain* of disease or infection; it was *work* for a good. It was not a problem to be avoided; it was the hard work of pure love. It was a process. Each wave was visualized as the most powerful muscle in the body pushing forth a new child of God into the light of independent life. It was a demonstration of strength, reframing *pain* into *work*.

In the decades since that delivery, there have been times I've felt invited to reframe. Sometimes I've wanted to join the cast of *Monte Python's Flying Circus* and scream at the top of my lungs, "Run Away! Run Away!" But, when I couldn't or chose not to run away, the lessons I learned were profound.

When we move into the most difficult times, swim in the currents of uncertainty, fear, and anxiety, we can be given new sight, if our vision shifts to find growth in ourselves and others. Reframing helps.

In the Catholic tradition, our liturgy is a type of reframing. Instead of a funeral, we call it the Mass of Christian Burial, focusing on the promise of resurrection or what God does for us, rather than eulogizing the dead, what that person did for God. (There is an appropriate time at the Vigil the night before, to gather and tell stories, helping listeners recall the best of the deceased.) The liturgy before burial reframes the event and focuses the participants on the promise of resurrection.

Several years ago, I attended such a Mass for a teenaged boy. Just before the closing blessings, his mother stood to speak to weeping family members, friends, and dozens of pews filled with his classmates. She spoke clearly and carefully, telling us how much she knew she would never go through a single day without missing him, but she reminded us of a truth as she reframed her anguish, to be grateful to have known him. She had the privilege of being his mom for 17 years, filled with gratitude for his adoption, for hearing his laughter, and for sharing his joy—17 years of gratitude. That is powerful reframing. Her words consoled us; her loss of the future was embraced by her gratitude for the past.

Letting go of things we cannot control helps us to focus on what we can control. We do have control over one thing: our choice of how to react. We can adjust our attitude and our responses to anything, including unspeakable evil.

That is no excuse to allow evil to continue; I can join in campaigns against it. I may not be able to alleviate poverty, but I can support agencies and leaders whose work reduces it. I may not be able to eliminate prejudice and religious fanaticism from the whole world, but I can work for justice in my teaching and writing. I can help to reframe the real stories, bring truth to light, whenever possible.

Anger, I was taught, comes from fear of losing something, of anticipatory grief. Our world seems to be in a time of such grief. Old established power structures of white privilege are screaming and tweeting their anger and fears, focused on blaming anyone except themselves. We must focus on the hard work of bringing birth to change, to hope, to a kinder way of life and justice for all. We must reframe our world, overcome hatred and "otherness," and invite the world with the light of love.

PONDER . . .
How have you been able to reframe occasions of grief, fear, or anger so that you might have gratitude, love, and hope?

RESILIENCE AND PERSISTENCE

In the Taoist tradition, there is a lovely story about a man whose horse ran away. The villagers pitied him for his bad luck, but the man never gave up hope. A week later, the horse returned with a group of wild horses, and the villagers congratulated him on his good fortune. A month later, one of the wild horses he was riding threw him into a ditch; his leg was broken. Again, the villagers thought he had bad luck. Finally, soldiers came from the emperor's army to draft all the healthy men in the village. With his broken leg, he was left behind. Sometimes, we must wait awhile to see if our *luck* will change; by trusting that every setback is potentially temporary, we learn resilience.

I learned three lessons in persistence when I was a chaperone on whitewater rafting trips in West Virginia on the New River. You might recall my earlier story about the mystic peregrine falcon I discovered on that trip. What I did not write about was that I was apprehensive because of a near-death drowning experience I'd had in high school. My fear and dread of swift river currents were based on my very real memory. I knew that plenty of people died on those kinds of trips, even if they wore the best life jackets.

I took every precaution to avoid foolishness. In my meeting with the parents, I warned (read, *threatened*) them that if their children misbehaved and created any danger for their fellow students, they would pay to have their children airlifted out of the Red River Gorge by helicopter and brought back to Louisville before facing disciplinary action. I wasn't messing around; my three-year-old self from her grandfather's Studebaker was at the ready. My fears soon were relieved by a successful trip and what I learned about persistence.

The first morning dawned with the promise of lovely weather. Our guide was a handsome, confident, experienced leader who covered safety issues at the campsite, again at the supply cabin, and a few times before and after we launched our rafts. Lesson 1: "Listen to your Guide."

An automatic reaction to rough water is to let go of the paddle, to try to hold on to the raft. In fact, that is the quickest way to find yourself overboard. The best way to stay in the raft is not to hold on to it, but to dig into the whitewater with your paddle. The ferocity with which I did so was enough to keep me firmly planted in the raft on that trip and eight other rafting trips in years to come. Lesson 2: "Dig in."

The last lesson was that we were all in that raft together. Our guide was in the back and could see what needed to be done, but we needed to watch-out for each other, too. When we cooperated and paddled in sync, following the guide's instructions, we had a terrific time. Lesson 3: "Stick together."

Listen to your guide. Dig-in. Stick together. This white-water rafting philosophy helps me to face the most difficult circumstances, with persistence.

———————————— ◇ ————————————

PONDER . . .
**What philosophy of life helps you in times of fear, loss, or pain?
How have you been resilient and persistent?**

PHOTOGRAPHS AND THE UNKNOWN

My picture sits on a living room shelf of a young woman in India. I do not know her name, and I do not have a photograph of her. We met at the Athirappilly Falls in the Thrissur District of Kerala, India on the Chalakudy River. She was a young pilgrim with short black hair and deep brown eyes. She asked to take my photo, and while it surprised me, I agreed after Father John explained the customs.

Her short hair indicated that she had only recently cut it off as a symbol of religious devotion, a quest for a threshold toward divine revelation. My photo would be a way to remember and introduce her American friend to visitors in her home. I found it unusual; I barely have photos of friends, except in scrapbooks. I certainly don't keep photos of unknown people on my mantle. But somewhere I sit in the home of my unknown Indian friend. It's all about connection, belief in that connection because of our belief that God connects us all.

Shortly after we invaded Iraq, there was a news articles with a black and white photograph of a little boy sitting on the side of the road. Alone, he was waiting with two large bags, presumably holding his family's belongings. They were fleeing their home.

I was so struck by this little fellow. He somehow looked familiar, with his dark hair, fair skin, and a faraway look in his precious eyes. He wore jeans, a shirt with a little vest, and tiny sneakers. I cut the picture out of the newspaper and placed it in the window of my office door, so I would remember to pray for him every day. He is in my heart. If he survived emigration and war, he must be in his 20s now. Have my prayers for him ever made a difference in his life?

$\diamond$

PONDER . . .
Do you have photos of people whose names you've forgotten, but memories remain? Do you celebrate the friendship like my pilgrim friend from India or feel the sadness like my grief for the little boy from Fallujah?

A "THIRD WAY"

In J. Milburn Thompson's book *Justice and Peace: A Christian Primer*, he explains a passage in the gospels about "turning the other cheek." It has always been a challenge to imagine that Jesus was telling his followers to allow themselves to be beaten up. It sounds masochistic, creating martyrs. But that isn't the point. Thompson explains that we think of only two choices, fighting or allowing ourselves to be beaten up by an aggressor, but there is a *third way* of understanding the passage. It is a culturally rooted explanation which makes sense.

In the Ancient World, a master would discipline a servant by hitting him in the face with the back of the right hand; the inside of the hand was used to caress, not to hit. Imagine if you were facing someone who was going to hit you with the back of his right hand, instead of giving him the right side of your face, you would turn your head to present the left side. He would be unable to strike; he'd have to adjust his stance, shift to the other back hand. With this adjustment, he'd find himself off balance. In other words, he'd have to think about what he was doing, slow down, and maybe spare your face. "Turning the other cheek" doesn't mean that you allow yourself to be assaulted; it means that you throw the aggressor off balance.

Sometimes we face situations where we feel nonphysical aggression. Three years before my retirement I learned how to use *third-way* thinking in such a case. How I wish I had known it long, long ago.

One of my friends, Denise used to say, "Never complain and never explain." I understood and agreed with the complaining part well enough. But the explaining part made sense when I was involved in a training session with fellow chaplains. The instructor taught us about handling accusations, especially when we were being accused of something we did not do or say.

Most of us move into a defensive mode, attempting to explain ourselves, to clarify or add details to the story to force our accuser to see the full truth. We are trying to fight back; it rarely works. The best defense is to look a bit confused and say, "I don't know what you are talking about."

This forces your accuser to repeat the story he has heard about you. You know it isn't true, but if you can persist in forcing him to explain himself, he loses steam. It plants just the tiniest seed of doubt that maybe he doesn't have all his facts straight. As you continue to look confused, he must do a little more homework. You don't apologize for anything or explain it away. It's now his problem.

PONDER . . .
Have you ever been wrongly accused of something and wondered how the facts became distorted, forcing you to try to explain? What did you do?

REPENTANCE

Throughout Covid, I've taken long walks almost every morning. It's not a particularly challenging walk, but the routine of seeing the same trees and squirrels each morning gives me some comfort. The silence of the early day, the chirping of the birds, and the way in which the natural world seems to be totally unaffected by the lockdown is especially poignant. It reminds me of another interpretation of the Garden of Eden story.

Fr. Ron (Catholic priest) completed a doctorate in ministry with McCormick Theological Seminary, a Presbyterian school of theology in Chicago where his commencement speaker was a Baptist minister. In

AN APARTMENT NEXT TO THE ANGELS

this ecumenical setting, the speech focused on sin. The minister pointed out that while we list sins in the plural, there actually is only one sin— the refusal to be human.

There are two manifestations of this refusal, either acting unaware of the human cost, the morality of our behavior, or acting as if we think we are God. Instead of letting God be God and humans be humans, we act without thinking carefully of possible consequences. Those consequences must be addressed for us to be healthy, well-integrated humans. Whether we name them as *sins* or not, we make mistakes, hurt others, and destroy relationships by your actions. What do we do about it?

During the Days of Awe in Judaism between *Rosh Hashanah* and *Yom Kippur*, Jews prepare for the latter, which means the "Day of Atonement." It is a time of *teshuvah* which can be translated as repentance, but its literal meaning is "to turn around, to return to a beginning." Some compare this to walking a labyrinth, with one way in and one way out. Not a maze, with dead ends, the path of the labyrinth invites us on a meditative walk, to focus and return renewed.

It reminds me of Thomas Merton again, the notion that in acknowledging our shortcomings and sins, we repent and return to our "true self." He wrote that our false self is not real; it is illusion. Our false, sinful self isn't even recognized by God because that self does not exist. He adds, "To be unknown to God is altogether too much privacy" (Merton, *New Seeds*, 34).

Throughout his papacy, Pope Francis has reminded us that this is what our God of mercy does. God sees us as we truly are and invites us to return to our best selves. We are brought back into loving arms.

PONDER . . .
When was the last time you had to apologize for something? How do you repent (apologies, sacramental confession, or a day of atonement)?

MY WAKE

In 2001, I'd just begun my full-time role in campus ministry and had barely unpacked the office supplies for my desk when I was visited by a faculty member who told me that one of our nontraditional students had died. We needed to attend the funeral, scheduled in an hour. The funeral home was 25 minutes away; there was no time to think.

When we arrived at the funeral home, I realized that I really was out of my element. Most of the mourners were in denim jackets and leather pants. Our student had clearly been an active motorcyclist. We made our way up to the coffin and stopped for a silent prayer, introduced ourselves, and expressed our condolences to the family. We sat near the rear of the chapel. Someone stood to say something; a preacher shared a scripture passage, which I don't remember; and, a boom box, turned to maximum volume, playing Norman Greenbaum's "Spirit in the Sky."

If you are a fan of *The Wizard of Oz* movie, you'll remember Dorothy saying, "This isn't Kansas anymore!" No truer words described that day for me. It was nothing like any funeral I had ever attended; the music was a complete surprise compared to the hymns of most funerals, but I knew that I wanted that song at my wake. Shocking to my family and friends, it is likely to be. But there it is.

When Mom died, her seven children were gathered near her coffin, checking to make sure they hadn't overdone her makeup. (They had.) As we walked into the chapel for the visitation, there was some nondescript, funeral instrumental playing; we stopped in our tracks. "No way," I thought. My two youngest siblings and I simultaneously said that what we needed was Herb Alpert and the Tijuana Brass. Our liaison found the exact album cover we described and put it on a loop. Mom's friends smiled or laughed at how perfect the music was!

I knew what I needed to do. After finishing the plans for my Catholic Mass of Christian Burial, I made a list of upbeat and fun music for my Visitation/Wake, including "Spirit in the Sky."

There will be a vast selection of jazz, chosen by Sean, our musician. On the rest of the list, from the 1960s to today, there are soothing melodies and unexpected rhythms, many heavy on bass and percussion. I want Louis Armstrong and the Dave Clark Five, Mozart and the Moody Blues, Gershwin and Sondheim, Gilbert and Sullivan, Vivaldi and Credence Clearwater; Bach and Burt Bacharach, Tchaikovsky and the Beatles—my favorite classics.

I've thrown in a few for fun including the Hollie's "Long, Cool Woman in a Black Dress," Blue Oyster Cult's "The Reaper," and Pink Floyd's "Another Brick in the Wall." For more nostalgic memories, I included "Cecilia" by Simon and Garfunkel and John Denver's "Country Roads."

When I was the registrar for the art museum, we hosted a photography competition for which the judge was collector and famous singer/songwriter, Graham Nash. I had many efficient things to do for the show, and I tried to stay quietly in the background, but I was certainly starstruck. I don't remember anything he said to me, only that he was terribly nice. So, my last two songs on the list are "Southern Cross" and "Teach Your Children" by Crosby, Stills, Nash, and Young.

PONDER . . .
What songs do you associate with happy times in your life: dances, your first crush, college after-game parties, or falling in love? If your tradition allows, what songs will you have played at your wake to remind your friends of you?

INTO THE GREAT UNKNOWN

Besides the upbeat songs I want at my wake, I've prepared selections for my final Mass, that express my personal faith. They include Bernadette Farrell's setting of the *Magnificat*, Dan Schutte's setting of Ignatius Loyola's *Suscipe* prayer, "These Alone Are Enough," and "Lord of All Hopefulness" by Jan Struther set to the Irish tune, *Slane* (accessible on YouTube). I encourage you to do the same planning in your tradition. In thinking about our earthly end and how we wish to be remembered, there is one other exercise I've used with students on discernment retreats: Write your epitaph.

This book has been a time for you to recall much of what you have experienced as you've "lived the dash." In her poem entitled, "The Dash," Linda Ellis has defined it as what comes between your birth date and death date on your tombstone. How can you summarize that dash? What quote or prayer or idea will you have engraved on it?

It can be serious or whimsical. My friend Denise says that hers will read, "I hate it when this happens!" One of my students told me she would have "No matter where you go, there you are" engraved on hers. I used to say that mine would be: "Wait, I still have 500 hours of comp time left!" If you want a longer assignment, write your obituary to see what and who have mattered to you most in this life.

Sacred Presence,
Thank you for the times you have helped me to cultivate resilience,
to reframe all that frightens me or that leaves me paralyzed.
Thank you for the gift of hope in a future with you
and with those I've loved who have gone before me.
Amen.

9

Purple Fragments

Accepting Unresolved Issues

When I am an old woman, I shall wear purple.
—from "Warning" by Jenny Joseph

When I worked in the art museum, we had the loveliest docent who wore only shades of purple. She made her donations in purple ink on lavender checks, and used a purple tint on her white hair, before it was fashionable. She was a retired teacher who had adopted the poem partially quoted above, as her retirement philosophy. Forbidden to wear purple in her youth because it was considered risqué, in her senior years, she could do whatever she wanted to do. (Look for the poem on the internet; you won't be disappointed.)

Besides the freedom of age described in the poem, there is a freedom that comes from accepting the unknown and what we cannot change. Regular spiritual practice teaches me to breathe and to trust, because there are many things I am not meant to know or resolve. Even so, there are ideas with which I still wrestle, so for this chapter, I am going to wear the purple of the poem, to push a bit against the status quo.

I have gathered a few fragments from the past five years of thinking and writing into this penultimate chapter, to share a few last thoughts. This chapter brings my spiritual legacy to a close because Chapter 10 is filled with voices from others whose struggles led them to walk away.

WHAT NO LONGER SERVES

For the last couple of years, I have spent a monthly Sunday afternoon with a group of women in a New Moon Circle. Organized by the Spirit of Sophia, a women's spirituality network and inspired by the writings of Dr. Christine Page, they created a ritual which allows us to "release what no longer serves us" and embrace the new month's promise without the weight of unnecessary emotions, or unrealistic expectations. Afterall, discernment covers both walking toward and away.

There are a few topics that still cause me to fuss and shake my finger like the 3-year-old Melanie who admonished her grandfather for braking so quickly. Most often, those topics are about injustice, unfairness, inequity, exclusion, or exceptionalism—any suggestion that people are unequal because of their gender, ethnicity, religion, worldview, orientation, or complexion.

My spiritual legacy would be incomplete without addressing some of those triggers. Some bring anger intertwined with fear, subtle messages that so many women sense of not being good enough, strong enough, smart enough, or pretty enough. They may only be a search for balance, for what I think is God's justice.

◇

PONDER . . .
What are some issues that make you feel anger or distress? How do you seek balance between the positive and negative forces in your life?

WORKING FOR JUSTICE

In our Hebrew classes, we learned to begin with the root letters and to explore other words associated with those same roots. When we look at one word in English, we can explore many definitions of a word to bring us deeper into the text, too. For instance, when I write the word "justice," what do you think about? Many of my students thought of criminal justice or punishment. But the word "just" means "fair or balanced." Recalling your theology exercise in Chapter 1, how is your God just?

As I read Merton's *Conjectures of a Guilty Bystander*, it reminded me of Edmund Burke's quote in the 18th century: "The only thing necessary for evil to triumph is for good people to do nothing." It could easily have been on Sister Cyprian's mind, when she showed us the films of the liberation of the concentration camps, which moved me toward my lifelong interest in and study of Judaism, anti-Semitism, acute injustice.

In my university ministry days, Fr. Ron articulated our mission, "We are consciously Christian; deliberately Catholic; and, unapologetically ecumenical and interfaith." He helped us define "catholic" (Greek, *kata holos*, "according to the whole") to understand the term as "universal and inclusive." We welcomed all without being defensive of that stand. It didn't please everyone, but it helped us to work for a justice of inclusion.

I believe that we are all called to some form of justice work. Some of us are called to demonstrate; others, to write letters. Some of us make the sandwiches for those who are building the Habitat for Humanity houses or serving the homeless under the bridges of our city. Some people run for political office to try to create systemic change, while others chant and pray for us in monasteries, sending their spiritual energy toward just causes and those who work for them. Each of us must discern justice work.

One of my favorite champions of social justice is Sr. Helen Prejean, best-selling author of *Dead Man Walking* and her inspirational autobiography, *River of Fire*. She's been a mentor to me for over 20 years as she has shared her stories through a lifetime of discernment. As a Sister of St. Joseph, she is well-versed in Ignatian spirituality, using discernment language fluently. When I've had a difficult decision, she has been able to remind me to search for the peace (consolation) that comes with doing or choosing the right thing.

One day, Sr. Helen told me that she had been approached about using her influence to push forward a particular women's issue. More than a few of our friends are passionate about this issue, but Helen was able to explain to them that she *knows* that she is called to persist in her work to abolish the death penalty. If she were to split her energies toward any other cause, she would not be following *her* call or be true to herself.

PONDER . . .

How do you discern the calls to justice in your life? How have you been just or fair to yourself and found peace after saying a firm, but gentle, "No. Thank you"?

INCLUSIVE LANGUAGE

He. He. He. Let me be frank. I am tired of male language in the Catholic liturgy. Honestly, "tired" is a politely disguised euphemism for "frustrated and disgusted." When only male pronouns are used to refer to God and only male images of the community persist, I feel left out.

For several years, we had been looking forward to a new translation for our Catholic prayer book, the *Third Roman Missal*. Several campus ministers hosted a day for students across Kentucky to review it. When we reached the new translation for the Creed, the ancient prayer that outlines what we profess to believe, one young woman expressed her profound distress at the phrase "for us men and our salvation." She felt left out of this community proclamation of faith at every Sunday and Feast Day Mass.

In response, I suggested that what she might want to do was to pause, simply to breathe within the phrase, to say, "for us," take a breath and then say, "and for our salvation." Within a split second, a young man interrupted to say that I was *not* allowed to do that. He said that to change the Creed was heretical, and I had no right to do so.

I explained that it is a very long statement of faith, one which requires us to pause to breathe quite often, and that I was merely suggesting *when* she might breathe. That didn't satisfy him. I tried to make small talk with him during our break, but I'd obviously alienated him. It saddened me, but I was more focused on helping women navigate the way we feel dismissed.

Thankfully, there is more to this story. About three years later, I received an email from the young man who reintroduced himself as the one who had "refused to allow the young woman to breathe during the Creed." Without any details, he assured me that in the time that had lapsed, many things had happened in his life and that he now understood. "I get it," he wrote. Stunned, I responded quickly with thanks, telling him that I would print his email to read every time I found myself feeling like a failure (or heretic). Sometimes, grace arrives after delay, a reminder that God isn't finished with any of us, yet.

To be perfectly fair, many of my priest friends were equally disturbed by the translation. They have no more power than we do over the hierarchy. For example, my pastor, Fr. Randy, always preaches about God's love, God's mercy, and God's grace. In over 11 years, I've never heard him reduce God to the male pronoun—not once.

PONDER . . .
How have you addressed issues of inequity in language?

STABILITY

In *An Encouraging Word*, Fr. Ron wrote that when we were baptized, the words used are "in the name of the Father, the Son, and the Holy Spirit," what our Catholic tradition teaches is a community of persons, one Trinitarian God. Those words bring us into Divine community, and he advised readers to refrain from thinking of the Church as a mere institution. He invited those who feel frustrated not to *abandon* the community (187). That is a compelling invitation to me, even though I know many of my friends who have left, have done so with careful consideration, as their stories explain in Chapter 10.

Just as compelling to me is a quote from Eileen Flanagan, "Wrestling with your tradition, including its scriptural texts, is a way of being in profound relationship with it. Rather than being disrespectful, it means taking it seriously, acknowledging its strength" (Flanagan, 41). I hope that my discomfort with some of the Church's teachings and liturgical language indicate that I've given my faith careful consideration. Still, you might ask why I stay. My response is "spirituality and identity."

I love the rituals, the miracles, and the stories of holy women and men in my tradition. Sometimes at Mass, I feel as if I am with the apostles and their wives in the Cenacle. This feeling is both a Jewish and a Catholic concept: certain rituals connect us across time and distance. At a Passover Seder, we are all with Moses as he left Egypt to cross the desert. At Mass, we are all with Jesus and Mary Magdalene.

By Catholic *identity*, I mean the family ties with women like my earliest teachers, the Marianites of the Holy Cross. I stay because of Sr. Helen; because of my cousin, Sr. Camille and the Sisters of the Eucharistic Covenant in Louisiana, with whom I am an Associate; because of the Franciscan Friars of India who now serve in Louisville; because of the Benedictine Sisters and Monks who have been my professors and spiritual directors; because of the women of the Margaret Beaufort Institute of Theology; because of my late uncle, Brother Austin Bourgeois, FSC; because of my priest friends like Fr. Ron, Fr. Damo, Msgr. Mark, and Fr. Dominic; and because of great spiritual writers from Julian of Norwich to Elizabeth Johnson. They are my Catholic family, as close in spirit as my faithful 18th century and more recent Acadian ancestors, my siblings, and their children. Family identity is important to me.

Being a Préjean means a lot to me. After our son, Sean, was born, I faced a serious decision about adopting Sullivan as my last name. I thought we ought to be a family with the same surname, but I didn't want to give up Préjean. Hyphenating Préjean with Sullivan seemed like too many syllables. I decided to hyphenate my birth name, instead. Sean once explained to a young friend, "Sullivan is our family name, but my mom is a Préjean."

My feelings about the Catholic church are very similar. My identity isn't tied to an institution; it is based upon the essential teachings of a Jewish rabbi in the 1st century CE about interconnection and love. The Vatican doesn't determine my identity.

My spiritual growth and development in the last few years have been steeped in two "charisms" or "spiritualities" that keep me grounded in my own faith. With the Sisters of the Eucharistic Covenant, I attempt to live their charism: to practice radical hospitality, to live in gratitude, to seek the holiness in all people and creation, and to be transformed by these actions (Sullivan, *Eucharistic Imagination*, 4–5). With the Benedictines, I have studied the *Rule of St. Benedict* from which I have learned about the vow of stability. You might compare it to, "bloom where you are planted" in secular thinking. I use it to encourage myself to persist, even when I feel like running away.

FIDELTY

When I was teaching the discernment class, I set aside several days to discuss marriage. I asked my students how they would handle falling in love with someone *after* they were married. I shocked them! One young man was visibly upset and said, "Well, I guess I'd have to get a divorce." I asked the class for an alternative solution. You could hear the crickets; they had no clue.

One student said that he thought if he fell in love with someone and married her, then he would never be tempted by anyone, ever again. I suggested that he sounded a bit superstitious, that a vow and a ring could magically make him faithful and protected from any temptation. The class discussion shifted to the difference between being *in love* and choosing *to love*, comparing the energy of the former to the intentional commitment of the latter. In my experience, being in love was like an energy that you could learn to channel.

I told them the story of the young nun who went to her Mother Superior in tears because she felt that she had to leave convent life. She had fallen in love. "Oh that," said the Mother Superior. "I've fallen in love three or four times in my life, but I didn't act upon the feelings. I learned to channel that energy into my vocation. Being a nun means more to me than any man."

We had a long discussion in class about how we can channel our energy away from situations which might lead to indiscretions, like avoiding alcohol or being alone with anyone besides their spouses. By the end of the class, they had lots of ideas about how to be careful at conferences or conventions, where there are hotels and anonymity. They figured it out.

About fidelity, the women of the Margaret Beaufort Institute of Theology in Cambridge have taught me about "double minority status" and all that entails—as women and Catholics in England. Their fidelity to their mission is inspiring. Their associates from all over the globe have given me a truly Catholic perspective, a bigger picture, much less parochial than I had before my sabbatical. They offered me a safe space to ponder, question, and dream. In their faithful witness, they offered me a chance to be my Catholic self with them.

PONDER . . .
Where and how have you remained faithful to your true self?

SCARCITY THEOLOGY

In our most serious decisions, fear sometimes blocks our clear thinking. Fred, a chaplaincy colleague, taught me about the fear of having too little, or "scarcity theology." Based upon the idea that only a *few* people will be saved, it creates an impression that there is *too little* of many other things.

If heaven is limited, God becomes a jealous, judgmental, greedy tyrant with a tiny mansion in paradise only a few will enter. A tiny heaven suggests everything is limited; it must be hoarded and protected from those who look, think, or vote differently.

That means that no immigrant or "other" deserves the "good stuff." Sadly, I think this is where we are in America today. Such a bigoted, selfish, fearful attitude is like a virus that grows exponentially; I find it just as frightening as Covid.

I find many who are opposed to more liberal immigration policies, more racial justice initiatives, and of course, any expansion of women's rights or leadership are those with fear at the basis of their thoughts. It is a fear of *too little*.

At Evensong in the Lady Chapel at Ely Cathedral, I sat surrounded by a magnificent stone frieze of bas-relief statues of angels, saints, and martyrs. Hundreds of these spiritual mentors had been decapitated by religious zealots during the English Reformation. Sitting in prayer, I found it reminiscent of encounters I've had over the years with people who hold a conviction that their faith is the only true one, and the rest of us must be destroyed.

There is a portion of a matriculation blessing I found to pray in response. From St. Edmund's College in Cambridge, it begs protection against fears which spiral into zealotry. It reads, "May we be delivered from fear before new truth, complacency before half-truth, and pride that would claim all truth."

PONDER . . .

How have you explained your opinions to people who you knew would never agree with you? Have you ever chosen to remain where people said, "If you don't like it, why don't you leave?" How do you maintain your integrity?

MULTIPLE PERSPECTIVES

In contrast to the fears of scarcity, I've learned a lesson from Judaism about abundant generosity. Third century rabbis recorded and maintained diverse opinions of a passage from the *Torah*, without deciding one was right and one was wrong. Their *Talmud* preserves these commentaries together. On a single page, a Torah passage is surrounded by multiple commentaries. It's beautiful. In adult Jewish learning settings, it continues as all are invited to add opinions— everyone. No one is silenced.

As a Catholic, I grew up trying to force myself to accept only official interpretations of our scriptures. The Sisters were very open-minded, but even they had parameters around which they had to teach us religion. We were taught about heresies from the writings of those who condemned them, who had often destroyed the original texts. All we had were the quotes, attacked by their adversaries. Can you imagine taking three or four sentences of this book out of context, burning the rest, and accusing me of heresy? If I was important enough, it could happen. It is like history, written by the victors, who never tell the whole story, and conveniently omit the perspective of the loser.

Another remarkable gift from Judaism is *midrash*, imagining the rest of the story from a biblical text. What did Eve say to Adam, after they left the garden? How did Miriam feel about her gift of finding water in the desert? It takes spiritual imagination to a whole new level and embeds tremendous life lessons in an expanded understanding of what is hidden, what might have been, but was left out of the final scripture text. If you are intrigued, I refer you to Ellen Frankel's *The Five Books of Miriam: A Woman's Commentary on the Torah*. She helps reader to imagine what has been lost in the story.

I've tried *midrash* when studying Christian Scripture to imagine other perspectives. For example, consider Jesus' saying, "In my Father's house, there are many dwelling places" (John 14:2). Could these dwelling places refer to many religions? I consider it a significant text for interspiritual relationships. For a biological/forensic perspective, there are almost eight billion people on this planet today, and no two of them have the same fingerprints. We are all unique children of God. Why would God want us to be the same religion?

PONDER . . .
How have you imagined new answers to old questions or imagined the "rest of the story?"

TWO LOVES/THREE QUESTIONS

There is a poignant story in the Gospel of John in which Jesus asks Peter if he loves him. He poses the question three times. In the original Greek, the passage has two different words for *love*, even though there is only one in our English version.

Unlike in English, there are many words for *love* in Greek: *philia*, the love we have for our friends; *storge*, for members of our family; *eros*, for our lover, partner, or spouse; *philautia*, for ourselves; and *agape*, which Greek Christians used for selfless love, as God has for creation. It is a transcendent kind of love. In the first question of the gospel passage in Greek, Jesus asks Peter if he loves him, using the word, *agape*. Peter answers using a form of *philia*, the love between friends.

Jesus asks Peter a second time, still using the word *agape*, and Peter answers again using *philia*. Finally, Jesus asks Peter using the term *philia*. We can almost imagine Jesus' disappointment; he seeks a transcendent relationship with Peter but gets mere friendship.

It is often said that "all translations are treason" because the translator inevitably inserts personal perspective. Language is so powerful that studying biblical texts out of context can be very, very dangerous; it's where most fundamentalist religious stances originate. Knowing a bit more about original texts is one way to push back against those who want everyone to be the same.

PONDER . . .
Have any of the stories in this collection prompted you to see something from a new perspective, to broaden your outlook?

INTERSPIRITUAL CHAPLAINCY

Many of the essays in this book have been about lessons I learned from studying with people of all faiths and none. I offer another lesson I've learned from Judaism in the prayer called the *Shema*: "Hear O Israel, the Lord is our God. The Lord is One." *Shema* means "to listen." As I noted in Chapter 6, it also is the first word of the Prologue to the *Rule of St. Benedict*: "Listen. . . with the ear of your heart." (*Chittister*, 19). We must involve our whole selves in the listening and be open to new possibilities.

To explore this in class, I used an illustration of five little bean men and an elephant. The men were totally visually impaired, so when they described the elephant, they each interpreted what they encountered. The one at the trunk said it was a powerful snake; the one near the ears thought it was a boat with huge sails; the one at the front foot thought it was a tree; the one along the side said it was a leathery wall; and the one at the tail concluded that it was a rope. We all have limited vision, unaware of the totality of God. We can only speak about God using metaphor, like we explained to our Martian in Chapter 1.

About three months before my official retirement from university ministry, I was searching for a way to validate what I felt called to do next. I found a certification program for ordained Interfaith Chaplaincy, but it was too far away and too expensive for me to justify; it felt like just another degree. At the time, I was a member of a spiritual book study group composed of friends in the Cooperative Baptist Fellowship (Progressive). As the only Catholic in the group, I was sometimes asked to explain theological concepts from my perspective and to invite them to do the same.

At our last meeting before my retirement, they asked me to explain why I felt the need for outside affirmation of my call. These thoughtful women suggested I might be over influenced by my Catholic understanding of hierarchical ordination. In their tradition, the community recognized gifts and ordained a leader. They asked me to explain what the title meant to me.

The word "chaplain" comes from the story of St. Martin of Tours in the 4th century. Martin encountered a beggar, but because Martin had no money and the poor man was freezing, he took out his sword and split his cape in half to share. His half cape became a symbol of generosity and charity. After Martin's death, it was housed in a small room near the church where it was guarded as a sacred relic. The keeper of this treasure, with the key to this little room for the cape (*chapel*), was called the chaplain. The story was meaningful to me for two reasons.

My paternal grandmother was a Martin, and I was the keeper of the keys to our university chapel, a privilege I treasured and took very seriously.

In my retirement, I further explained, that as an interfaith and interspiritual chaplain, I felt called to work especially with people in blended faith relationships, to teach about pluralism and welcoming the religious other. My Baptist friends announced that they were going to ordain me. I knew I was called to this life, to this ministry, but they knew I needed outside confirmation. While my devout Catholic friends sit in horror at this notion, it was a genuinely lovely gesture. From then on, I have used interspiritual chaplain to describe who I am.

My Catholic students kept me sharp in our social justice work and in remembering the full spectrum of practitioners of our faith, from very progressive to radical traditionalists. Jewish students taught me about *tikkun olam*, "healing the world." Muslim students taught me about the many names of God and the importance of fasting. Hindu students showed me their many manifestations of the One God. Buddhists helped me to accept that life is difficult unless I practice detachment. Pagan students taught me about reverence for all creation and why they do not make promises; because we cannot know the future, we never want to be guilty of a lie. Agnostic, atheist, and spiritually independent students taught me to think and not to judge. Christian students of all persuasions were living evidence of the continued splintering from schisms and reformations resulting in hundreds of interpretations of one testament. Unitarian Universalist and Baha'i students showed me how much all religions have in common.

PONDER . . .
What have you learned from people of other faiths?

WHAT IF?

American writer and fellow Catholic, Flannery O'Connor once said, "I write because I don't know what I think until I read what I say." To me, this is an excellent reason for journaling. It helps me to distill and to clarify what I'm thinking, especially after I've read something. I know that I might change my mind tomorrow or refine my thoughts next week, but by writing I gain new insights.

Within the Jewish-Hasidic tradition, there are many tales from which I've gleaned spiritual insight. One story to describe the work I think I'm doing is about a preacher who came into a village and told people to put

God into their lives. He repeated this often, until the local rabbi said, "God is already in there. Our task is simply to realize that."

In conversations with friends and colleagues who are not Christian, I'm often asked what I believe about Jesus, especially how can I believe in the Trinity and profess to be a monotheist. I answer that I think the last phrase of the Jewish prayer the *Shema*, "The Lord is One." is a perfect match for my overall creed. Julian of Norwich had a vision of this. She held a hazelnut in her hand and realized that the hazelnut existed only because God wanted it to exist, that God loved it into being and holds it there. God is One, holding us in existence. For me, God is ever present, constantly creating and saving. Operating in many capacities, God is still One.

When asked about Jesus as both God and human, I don't attempt ontological answers; I ask, "What if?" Think of the three types of learners: those who learn by listening, those who learn by seeing or reading, and those who learn by doing. What if God spoke to Abraham and Sarah (and to Buddha and Zoroaster) to teach them? Then, God had Moses write instructions for living a happy life: Respect God, who made everything. Rest once a week to be with God. Honor your mentors. Tell the truth. Respect life. Be faithful. Be grateful for what you have without worrying about what belongs to others.

Well, that covers *auditory* and *visual learners*. What about the third, *kinesthetic* learners, the ones who need a *hands-on* experience? Once there was a man who sat in the quiet dark of a winter storm, pondering what it meant to believe that God could become human. Suddenly, he heard the thumping of birds flying into his living room window, knocking themselves out. He decided to go out into the storm to his barn. He opened the doors wide and turned the lights on, so the birds would have a place to fly into safety. One or two birds flew in, but several remained in the whirling wind, flying into his house windows. "If only," the man said, "I could be a bird and show them the way to safety."

That's my simple theology of the incarnation; God decided that some of us needed to be *shown* the way, so God became human for about 30 years. Jesus came to teach us how to be human and how to be in relationship with God, not to start a new, exclusive religion.

PONDER . . .
How do you explain a difficult concept of your faith to friends of another faith?

OUR ULTIMATE END

When I think about heaven, I return to my libraries, to the first paragraphs of my Prologue. The memories of our little library at home and the ones throughout my studies assemble into an imaginary, mystical place. The books are joined by the people with whom I formed friendships and partnerships, all with stories and answers to my questions. That imaginary library, where books are never overdue and people join in quiet conversations, is my idea of heaven, what I hope for my afterlife. My husband's heaven might be a golf course, with no sand or water hazards. What's yours?

Discernment includes times to say, "Farewell," the focus of Chapter 10, with voices from others, instead of my own. In closing this chapter, I bring my spiritual legacy writing to a pause, but I hope you will join me in walking with those who discerned a different path. Meanwhile, may the lessons you learned about yourself continue to echo in your hearts and minds, bringing you energy to soar in your ongoing search, leading you to a place of peaceful non-knowing, and leaving your legacy for the next generation.

Sacred Presence is my light and my salvation;
whom should I fear?
Love is the stronghold of my life;
of whom shall I be afraid?
One thing I ask of God, this will I seek:
to live in God's house all the days of my life,
to behold God's beauty,
visiting and studying in God's Temple.
—*Psalm 27:1, 4* (Paraphase, mine)

10

Take Your Leave

Discerning What No Longer Serves

Calm and undisturbed, Benedict addressed them,
'It is impossible for me to stay here any longer.'
—Gregory (*Life and Miracles*, 11)

One of the most serious and frightening aspects of living a life of discernment is knowing that sometimes we will discern we must walk away from what was comfortable. I overheard a recent conversation my son had with one of his students, when he advised his young protege, "When you have friends who ask you to do something you know is wrong, it's time to *get new friends*" (Emphasis, mine). Walking away from what we know toward an unknown is often very scary and sometimes very sad.

This final chapter follows a different format. It begins with a question posed to me in 2003 and ends with stories I've collected more recently. These stories are all for pondering, but there is only one *ponder* pause in this chapter.

WHY DO YOU STAY?

Three young women came into my office to ask for a serious, confidential conversation. Two of them turned to their third companion with nervous nods. She asked me, "Why do you stay? I mean, we would like to know why a gifted woman like you stays in a patriarchal church."

It's not that I hadn't considered other options, I explained. In my own search, I found that there is no perfect church. Being *Catholic* is part of my identity, even if I have serious issues with the institution. I addressed some of those in Chapter 9.

There are Catholics who would vehemently disagree with this. They would tell me that if I can't accept all the teachings of the *Sacred*

Magisterium, that I should leave—excommunicate myself. Well, I don't agree, and no amount of bullying is going to change that. I am who I am.

Those three students continued their own discernment, as they wrestled with staying or leaving, each in her own way. But, what of those who have been bullied by fundamentalist Catholics or other Christians? What about those who have been driven from their churches or those who simply walked away, unnoticed?

RISING NUMBERS

Current sociological research labels those who have left organized religion as either "nones" or "dones." The first term originated when higher education demographics indicated a growing number of young adults choosing "none" after the query about religious affiliation. The "dones" ("finished") are older adults who have left their first faith. Both numbers have been increasing exponentially in recent years. (There are numerous references online, for more information.)

For many, the term "none" sounded too negative, so it became "spiritual, but not religious" (SBNR), but even that has a negative tone. I prefer what Rabbi Rami Shapiro calls them instead, "spiritually independent" (*Perennial*). I've met many who identity with this idea.

To some friends and colleagues, these spiritually independent young adults are their children. They've provided Catholic/Christian education, encouraged them in sacramental preparations, worked with godparents, sponsors, teachers, and coaches. But they have left. Why?

Some left because of what I label "ministerial malpractice," where ministers (predominantly men) who professed a belief in a loving God, acted as judges, condemning the very children of God they were supposed to lead. Sitting before me in tears, there have been LGBTQIA students who felt unwelcome and unloved by their pastors, church communities, and families. They left those communities to join more welcoming Christian denominations, not unlike students who left racist churches to join multiethnic ones.

One young man left his church when he discovered that he loved the Catholic liturgy and sacramentals, like the rosary. It initially matched how he felt until he realized that as a Catholic gay man, he would feel as if he was on the periphery. So, he became an Episcopalian, finding his spiritual journey richer and feeling accepted for who he was.

Several students left church, entirely, without seeking another Christian denomination. It isn't that they rejected all teachings or spiritual practices, they merely stopped identifying with a religious label of any kind.

I could relate hundreds of similar "leaving stories," but I have chosen to share three from young adults and ten from older women. It's important that we come to know individuals and not simply wring our hands lamenting the statistics.

YOUNG ADULT STORIES

First young adult: The parents of one young adult divorced when she was in lower school, and her memories of their arguments still haunt her. She was sent to a Catholic school for her first few years, then to a Montessori school until high school. She recalls that the Catholic school "never allowed questions." Everything seemed fear-based; God was always angry with them for their mistakes (like divorce). In the Montessori school, she had been allowed—even encouraged—to question. It seemed to her that *love* was at the core. The school focused on being kind and treating people as you wanted to be treated. She really liked the atmosphere.

After the divorce, attending Mass was no longer a custom. She became a more scientific thinker, looking for provable answers for all her questions. As she turned to science, she found herself gradually leaving the Church's "black- and-white" thinking. High school "didn't help." She was in an all-girls Catholic school, which had "retreats and all kinds of religion classes," but she had already rejected most of what she was being taught. As an introvert and someone who loves learning, for her the questions and personal reflection were more important than the packaged answers she received.

In college, she discovered philosophy and studied other religions and spiritual practices. She learned Yoga and Buddhist meditation; she came to believe in the concept of energy being recycled. Mostly, she realized that each of us has our own interpretation of God, that we all have a spiritual self, which is centered within nature or creation.

Her ultimate question is still whether suffering is an intended part of the process. She wonders about the Hindu ladder of reincarnation. For now, she feels at one with nature. This is where she has spiritual experiences, not in a church.

Second young adult: Another young adult grew up in a Catholic family. His aunts, uncles, and cousins are numerous, but he is an only child and both parents are still together. He attended private and public grammar schools and an all-boys Catholic high school. For his primary religious education, he attended his parish Sunday school. He always thought he'd try to make the most out of a less-than-ideal situation (i.e., "having to go"). He had close friends at church, and his parish was open-minded with a theological worldview of an all-loving, nonjudgmental, forgiving God. He was always "pretty bored" in Mass, but the parish was very focused on social justice, and he experienced God in service. He liked the idea of being "God's hands" in the world. He traveled to Central America for service and felt God there among the poor and within the service group.

For him, the "Beatitudes" (Latin, *blessed are*) were more important than church rules. At least, they resonated with him, and what he believed was the Christ-message. In service, he found hope and satisfaction as if God was affirming him. He was part of his college's music liturgy program. But as much as he tried, he never really felt connected to God in Mass. It was never as meaningful as being in service to others.

Retreats were often inspiring, but in his "day-to-day spiritual journey," he finds God in music, friends, nature, and family. The institutional church leaves him cold and indifferent, especially since the scandals of abuse and coverup. Now that the Church in America seems to be politically so conservative, he wants nothing to do with it.

Third young adult: Another student visited me, well into the first semester of her junior year, in which she was studying "Judaic Thought" with a dynamic rabbi. She said that "all of a sudden, everything about Judaism was logical" and that her Christian Orthodox upbringing was no longer making sense to her. She felt traumatized because religion and ethnic identity were completely intertwined in her life, and she had no idea how she could separate the two. Her grandmother was "going to be absolutely livid" and just might shun her forever for these thoughts. What was she going to do?

By the time she completed her undergraduate studies and a year of graduate school, she had encountered other non-Christian traditions and begun to settle into a Unitarian Universalist Association (UUA). After a few months, even this wasn't completely comfortable; she missed many of the rituals of the Orthodox Church, its sense of community, family, history, and tradition. Sometimes, she attends a Holy Week service or a Christmas liturgy. Thankfully, that's one thing that the UUA seems to be very adept at, allowing people to be connected to more than just the UUA. It's home to many religiously blended families and individuals. This kind of "double belonging" is very attractive to many young adults who want to participate in religious communities, without having to identify with only one faith.

During one of my first meetings with the IFYC, I attended an educators' session. We were asked to identify ourselves and our religious affiliations. There were about 40 people in the room, most of whom were in their 20s and 30s, working on campuses. As they stood to introduce themselves, I heard 27 different faith identities, 27 out of 40. Most of them were hyphenated: Jewish-Buddhist; Agnostic-Hindu; recovering-Catholic, etc. Double belonging in this generation of young adults seems to be very prevalent in the interfaith community.

Some young adults have given up on the idea that any one institution helps them to find God. Some parents of this generation lament their leaving or changing affiliation. Others tell me that they are relieved: They are ready to leave, too, and these young adult children have given them permission!

STORIES FROM OLDER ADULTS

Intrigued by those who say they are finished or "done," I embarked on my own mini survey during our Covid lockdown, virtually interviewing 10 women who ranged in age from 40 to 75. I did not intend it to be an academic study, but a chance to invite them to tell their stories. Some of them had experiences which overlap and intertwine with the research, but for this essay, I invite you simply to listen with the "ear of your heart" to their stories.

Most were raised Catholic; others were part of other Christian denominations. Some had officially walked away from their churches, but some are "waiting" because they still have children or grandchildren for whom they feel a responsibility of formation. As one said, "I want them to have the same foundation that I had, so that they can choose to stay or freely walk away as adults, without feeling either guilt or as if they never belonged. Plus, all their cousins are this faith, and I want their pivotal sacramental moments to be celebrated by the family and to give them a sense of connection to something bigger."

One of the younger interviewees remarked that her middle-school son was questioning whether he would receive the sacrament of Confirmation because, "If the Church won't let our gay friends get married, then I don't want to belong to that Church." This coincides with studies which try to pinpoint key issues for Catholics leaving. For the baby boomers, it was the teaching on contraception; for current young adults, it includes teachings on gender identity, roles, and rights.

The senior Catholic women in my survey, expressed a consensus that they "have waited for over 50 years" to see the Church enact the reforms of the Second Vatican Council, to see equity for women, to work for ecumenical dialogue and interfaith fellowship instead of "circling the wagons." One remembers being enthusiastic and hopeful about the

Council documents in the 1970s with their focus on social justice, but most of them decided that "the patriarchy is just too much." They are tired of waiting for change, especially "justice for women."

When I told a retired priest friend about my project, he said that one serious problem is, "We've started to worship the Church instead of following Christ." He is not alone. Among his many friends who have been ordained for more than a half century, this is a common lament as they meet young radical/traditionalist (aka "rad trad") seminarians. You can sense a profound sadness about the future of the Church these older priests love. They are allies with women, but there aren't enough of them left.

One respondent remarked that it was becoming harder to attend parishes where the young priests want to regress to a time of "pray, pay, and obey." She sees the pompous, know-it-all character of some young priests as intolerable. "I'm so sick of them thinking that there is only one political issue. That's why we are in trouble in this country—narrow-minded people who can't see the big picture."

Another said, "I've been studying theology and religion since before these guys were conceived. How can they expect me to respect their dismissive attitudes?" One remarked that she walked out because of a homophobic homily. It's becoming easier for these senior women to walk away from these newly ordained men who want a "1950s Church with June Cleaver in pearls, cleaning the altar and keeping silent."

Three of the women had horrific stories about preachers or priests. One was raised in a "cult-of-the-preacher" Christian denomination, and it wasn't until she and her husband moved away from their hometown that they realized how much they had been brainwashed. She is still processing the trauma of lessons she had internalized until her adult questions brought her to a different truth.

Another woman was told by a priest that her daughter, who has a physical disability, was living a life "in sin" since she was clearly "not fully made in the image of God." She knows this to be untrue, but she feels conflicted with childhood memories of the fear of hell and feeling the need to exaggerate her own sinfulness in weekly confession to "cover any sins she forgot to count, in case I died on the way home from church." It wasn't unusual to seek the advice of older siblings about the mysteries of confession. The older brother of one woman told her to confess adultery—a 7-year-old! The priest was not amused.

Another had a similarly traumatic "first confession." After missing the religion class meetings because of a highly contagious childhood disease, she was pushed forward by a "clicker nun." (Some sisters used a small metal clicker to signal when to stand, to kneel, or for your row to move forward for something.) She was totally unprepared as she entered the confessional. Her tiny self was shocked to see that there was a "man hiding behind a screen" and she panicked. Dismissed with confusing instructions from the priest, she asked an older cousin what to say. He told her to say that it had been "25 years since my last confession." This priest knew exactly what had happened and was gentle in helping her.

But the sense of a rule-driven church with uncompromising, hidden, or coded rules never left her. Even the more progressive changes, explained in her high school religion classes left her confused. College ministry wasn't any more welcoming, and she went to graduate school still wondering what it was all about.

Several respondents pointed to the schizophrenic male God of their preachers: "One week He loved you and the next week He was going to send you to hell!" One respondent was raised in different churches as her family moved from an independent, conservative Christian denomination to a more mainline one. She was baptized at a revival following a "fire and brimstone" sermon, but gratefully encountered a minister at summer camp who was filled with a "sincere peace and joy." She knew she wanted that kind of faith.

Searching for decades, she even attended a seminary looking for answers. Studying feminist theology and learning about inclusive language helped, but she didn't find the worshiping community she needed. Realizing the weight of "hell theology," she sought a church without it and joined the UUA. It worked for many years until she moved to a small town without one. She is currently on a search for a community which speaks the language of the Divine Feminine.

After decades of male language for God, she wants to find the "Ancient Mother" in community and in nature: "Sometimes I hear her in the sounds of the babbling brook, the soft peaceful breeze of a forest, and especially in the chorus of birds that sing at dusk right before the complete silence at full darkness. The peace and joy I spent so many years searching for is not in a church building. I have discovered it at last, as I sit or walk contemplatively in nature be it garden, meadow, or forest."

For some respondents, church offered rituals and liturgies that were meaningful and spiritually "very nourishing." It was the overemphasis on dogma that drove them away. For some, it was an "us-versus-them" mentality leaving out women and nature, condemning all who didn't "follow the rules or who asked too many questions."

One woman traversed the path through Christian traditions from Baptist to no church to Catholic over several decades. As her children grew and she began to think more deeply about her questions, she realized that she was missing these same two things: women and nature. She tried several paths before she found two women's networks, one connecting to Divine Wisdom (a Catholic group) and one within an interfaith community, without any patriarchal oversight. Both groups view Wisdom as feminine, personified in Hebrew (*Chokmah*) and Greek (*Sophia*). These two communities of faith allow and even encourage questions.

One respondent grew up Catholic, "only about 100 yards from the Cathedral." She was married with four children when the teaching on contraception contributed to the collapse of her marriage. After a five-year process to obtain an annulment, she grew to understand herself and the Church more. She became convinced that she needed "to help change the Church." After degrees in psychology and ministry, she worked for the bishop, but "saw hypocrisy" that she had not anticipated.

After she left her job, she realized that Mass had become a meaningless habit. The institutional church felt "demeaning and destructive;" she needed to find another place. She continues to enjoy a solid spiritual support network, without church. She learned that "spiritual struggles have a reason, that God is good and so are many people who remain in the church." Many share the sentiment that its essence is still holy, even if its structure is not.

Becoming an agnostic for one respondent was a gradual process. As a senior woman, she embarked on a spiritual journey on her "bucket list." She studied Native American spirituality, Tibetan Buddhism, and both art and music therapies as paths to her own healing from a serious physical illness. She regularly uses guided meditation practices through which she finds great spiritual connection. She also meets regularly with a women's spirituality group.

Besides the need for physical healing, two respondents named the clergy sexual abuse scandal and coverup as their "tipping point," creating a sense of woundedness and need for emotional healing. One uses poetry as her creative outlet to express both her pain and healing.

Another very involved "cradle Catholic" experienced a personal crisis when news reports of a woman's testimony on Capitol Hill, which "was not believed," began to trigger flashbacks to her own abusive childhood. Coinciding with the clergy scandal, it was a time of near unraveling. Patriarchy in all forms was too much. She began to pull away from the church and no longer felt guilty about it. Her energies are now focused on book groups, which give her an opportunity to read and learn, to share, and to be heard. From metaphysics to self-help titles, she finds no bitterness, but a conviction that, "I had to learn to grow."

SPIRITUALITY OVER THEOLOGY

A common thread among many who have left organized religion is the realization that the answers are not found in church dogma, but in spirituality. They found connections to others and to nature, God's creations. They left institutions, but they found spiritual connections with those on similar paths.

The stories in this chapter allowed the tellers to be heard and appreciated, to be celebrated for their determination and courage. I wanted to prevent them from being mere statistics. This chapter might stir up many emotions from anger or defensiveness to outrage. In the end, I only wanted to include voices besides mine for us to consider.

PONDER . . .
Tell your own story about joining, staying, or leaving any community of faith. How are you currently caring for your own spiritual growth and connection to creation?

Let's consider the young adult's suggestion that the Beatitudes contain a vital message. Jesus teaches a way of facing problems, remembering we are not alone, that God's blessing are always with us. While there are also promises of the future, I think it is more significant that he says, "Blessed *are*. . ." in the *present* tense to emphasize God's abiding presence and faithfulness. These are the Beatitudes in the Gospel of Matthew 5:3–11:

> Blessed are the poor in spirit, for theirs is the kingdom of heaven.
> Blessed are those who mourn, for they will be comforted.
> Blessed are the meek, for they will inherit the earth.
> Blessed are those who hunger and thirst for righteousness, for they will be filled.
> Blessed are the merciful, for they will receive mercy.
> Blessed are the pure in heart, for they will see God.
> Blessed are the peacemakers, for they will be called children of God.
> Blessed are those who are persecuted for righteousness' sake, for theirs is the kingdom of heaven.
> Blessed are you when people revile you and persecute you and utter all kinds of evil against you falsely on my account.

A FINAL WORD

This brings our journey to a close. We have examined our beliefs about the Sacred, and our relationships with such a presence and with others. We've encountered joy and pain; grief and anger; resilience and persistence. We've embraced the unknowable and considered how to reframe or change our perspective, discerning whether to stay or walk away from what no longer serves us. And, we have considered some joyful ideas about the afterlife and our family celebrations at our earthly end.

I hope you have engaged your imagination, learned a little about discernment and can appreciate the joys of interfaith work. I also hope you have found it a rewarding journey, filled with invitation to create your own spiritual legacy.

Great Spirit,
You created the Big Bang and sang the Universe into being.
You separated land and water; sky and sea.
Send us your wisdom to distinguish our choices, clearly.
Help us to expand our hearts and minds
as you did in the beginning.
In wisdom, help us to find our paths,
with courage to stay or to leave,
knowing you are wherever we are.
Thank you.

Acknowledgements

I have always loved libraries, large and small, for their hidden wisdom. However, it has been people who have taught me the most about what I needed to know to find my true self and to write this book: family, friends, mentors, teachers, students, and companions throughout my life and this book's journey. In the eucharistic spirit of gratitude, I am privileged to name them, without whom you would not be reading this.

First, I acknowledge the women (and men) of the Margaret Beaufort Institute of Theology for the sabbatical, naming me the "Cardinal Hume Scholar" in 2017 and giving me the time, space, and support for beginning my discernment toward retirement. Principals Oonagh O'Brien, Anna Abrams, and Sue Price graciously helped me to dream of this book and to persist in writing it. Amy Daughton and Ferdia Stone-Davis, Directors of Studies, led our merry band of Research Associates and Visiting Lecturers. Rosalie Ní Mhaoldomhnaigh is a blessed kindred spirit; her hospitality and wisdom are beyond superlative description. Sr. Pavlína Kašparová, OP was a weekly companion during these last two years as we completed our respective writing projects and is the artist of my cover. Two priests associated with the institute were also great supporters of my endeavors: Fr. Dominic White, OP and the late, beloved Msgr. Mark Langham.

Bellarmine University Vice-President Fred Rhodes and the late President Joseph J. McGowan were generous supporters of campus ministry. Fr. J. Ronald Knott, my partner in that ministry for over 16 years, continues to be a mentor, friend, and cheerleader. His persistence in paying attention to his own growth, his dedication to his own writing, and his encouraging homilies helped me through countless challenging and rewarding experiences leading to this endeavor.

The late Archbishop Thomas C. Kelly, OP once corrected me when I told him that I loved working for him. He said that I did not work *for* him, but *with* him. On the day he placed the keys to the chapel in my hands, I knew he had confidence in me. We weathered more than a few storms together, and he first called me "chaplain," even when his fellow bishops argued about whether laywomen were permitted to use that title. May he rest in peace.

Elizabeth Hinson-Hasty has been a mentor and faithful companion from the first chapter to the last. She offered sage advice about focusing on my audience. She's made me a better teacher and a better writer by her example and personal dedication to both vocations.

From Paula Taylor, I learned to face my fears. From Laurie Doctor, I learned to write my own script. Thank you to Laura Kline, my talented companion in campus ministry and to Friars John Pozhathuparambil, OFM, George Munjanattu, OFM, Antony Vattaparambil, OFM, Leo Payyappilly, OFM, and Adam Bunnell, OFM, whose lives in the spirit of Francis of Assisi, always inspire. Thank you to Fred Ehrman, who taught me about scarcity theology and how to watch for "catastrophizing."

Sometimes you cannot realize your dreams where you are; you need outsiders to recognize and value your talents. Michael Galligan-Stierle knew about my dream of becoming a mission officer. Though we knew it would not happen where I was, he invited me to be part of a national training seminar for mission officers on Catholic college campuses. This book began as a completely different project, but Michael was instrumental in helping me reshape it, to focus on it as a memoir of mission and purpose. I am indebted to him for his confidence in me.

Nine years ago, Deborah Slosberg and I began learning together. She taught me Hebrew and introduced me to commentaries on the books of the Torah. She invited me to create my own courses for Louisville Melton, and she was the first to suggest that this book was an "ethical will." We've forged a friendship of mutual encouragement. Fellow Melton learners, Jane Goldstein and Helen Sweitzer, made sure that I didn't table the idea of writing the book when I almost gave up. They deserve much of the credit for the energy I needed to persist.

Eboo Patel and the Interfaith Youth Core conferences, publications, and training sessions were invaluable to my ministry and my personal formation as an interspiritual chaplain. Sr. Helen Prejean, CSJ with her sense of humor and passionate confidence in her vocation, passed on her enthusiasm from my first book on teaching discernment to this publication.

Thank you to those who participated in my research about leaving your religious traditions for new ones. It takes courage to make such a decision and more courage to share your stories. I am humbled by and grateful for your help.

Sisters Camille Martinez, SEC and Jeannette Touchet, SEC, in their annual invitations to present to Associates, created the atmosphere for telling stories and plumbing the depths of discernment. Fr. Damian "Damo" Dietlein, OSB taught me how to hear women's voices in Hebrew scriptures and the Septuagint. Sr. Karen Joseph, OSB helped me process my doubts and understand stability in the *Rule of St. Benedict*.

Professor Clayton Jefford taught me to pay attention to the text. Thank you to George Bonin who reminded me to pause and think carefully. The late, Professor Raymond Betts believed in me as a teacher. Rabbis Ari Ballaban and Sarah Tasman helped me to understand Jewish denominations and to appreciate interfaith encounters. Thank you to Mark Meade of the Thomas Merton Center and to Rev. Alan Race of the World Congress of Faiths.

My former students and colleagues at Bellarmine University and in campus ministry are too numerous to list here, lest I leave anyone unnamed. I learned from all of you. There are about a dozen of you with whom I have maintained close ties, and you know who you are. Thank you for teaching me and supporting my ideas so often.

To Mom and Dad, I acknowledge eternal gratitude. I am grateful to my siblings for allowing me to use their names and for helping to correct my memories. A special thank you to Andrea for your encouragement throughout the process, for serving as my first roommate, my best friend, a perfect traveling companion, a woman of great faith, and the heart of our Préjean generation.

Thank you again to Andrea, Jane, Fr. Ron, and Fr. Damo for giving me helpful feedback on the first draft. Thank you to Stephanie Hughes for your artistic advice. Heartfelt gratitude to Rebecca Kueber for your amazing desktop publishing talents. Thanks to the women of Alpha Delta Pi, Soul Sisters, and Spirit of Sophia, who have helped me to feel empowered, to experience what it means to have my voice heard and my dreams supported.

Thank you to Kevin for your constant love, affirmation, and encouragement. For over 44 years, you have believed in my abilities, even when I had doubts. You supported me with the flexibility to dream. To Sean, you have inspired and taught me since the day you were born to be a better person, to think deeper, and to love unconditionally. You are a talented musician and a great teacher. Thank you for being the best son any mother could have. To Kayci, my daughter-in-heart, thank you for your inspirational courage and feisty spirit, which enliven every family gathering and bring us such great joy.

References

Chip Andrus. (2010) "Psalm 133." *The Place We're At*, track 10. Lyrics used with permission.

Sophy Burnham. (1990) *A Book of Angels: Reflections on Angels Past and Present and True Stories*. New York: Ballantine.

Joan Chittister. (1992) *The Rule of St. Benedict: Insights for the Ages*. New York: Crossroad.

Eileen Flanagan. (2009) *The Wisdom to Know the Difference: When to Make a Chang and When to Let Go*. New York: MJF.

Ellen Frankel. (1996) *The Five Books of Miriam: A Women's Commentary on the Torah*. New York: HarperOne.

Estelle Frankel. (2017) *The Wisdom of Not Knowing: Discovering a Life of Wonder by Embracing Uncertainty*. Boulder, CO: Shambhala.

Viktor E. Frankl. (2000) *Man's Search for Meaning*. Boston: Beacon

J. Ronald Knott. (1995) *An Encouraging Word: Renewed Hearts, Renewed Church*. New York: Crossroad. See also his books through Sophronismos Press and his blog, https://revjrknott.blogspot.com/

Lawrence Kushner. (2001) *Jewish Spirituality: A Brief Introduction for Christians*. Nashville: Jewish Lights.

Wayne A. Meeks, Gen ed. (1993) *The HarperCollins Study Bible: New Revised Standard Version*. New York: HarperCollins.

Thomas Merton. (2009) *Conjectures of a Guilty Bystander*. New York: Image/Doubleday.

Thomas Merton. (1961) *New Seeds of Contemplation*. New York: New Directions.

Christine Valters Paintner. (2011) *The Artist's Rule: A Twelve Week Journey Nurturing Your Creative Soul with Monastic Wisdom*. Notre Dame, IN: Sorin.

Christine Page. www.christinepage.com

Eboo Patel (2016) *Interfaith Leadership: A Primer*. Boston: Beacon.

Eboo Patel (2012) *Sacred Ground: Pluralism, Prejudice, and the Promise of America*. Boston: Beacon.

Helen Prejean. (2019) *River of Fire: My Spiritual Journey*. New York: Random House.

Alan Race. (2021) *My Journey as a Religious Pluralist: A Christian Theology of Religions Reclaimed*. Eugene, OR: Wipf & Stock.

Richard Rohr. (2019) *The Universal Christ: How a Forgotten Reality Can Change Everything We See, Hope For, and Believe*. New York: Convergent.

Rami Shapiro. (2013) *Perennial Wisdom for the Spiritually Independent: Sacred Teachings: Annotated and Explained*. Woodstock, VT: SkyLight Paths.

Melanie-Préjean Sullivan. (2009) *Whispers, Nudges & A Couple of Kicks: A Guide for those who Teach and Practice Discernment*. Louisville, KY: Bellarmine University Press.

Melanie-Préjean Sullivan. (2020) "Eucharistic Imagination as a Paradigm for Practical Theology," *Practical Theology*, https://doi.org/10.1080/1756073X.2020.1783082.

Barbara Brown Taylor. (2018) *Holy Envy: Finding God in the Faith of Others*. New York: HarperCollins.

J. Milburn Thompson. (1997) *Justice and Peace: A Christian Primer*. Maryknoll, NY: Orbis

J. Bradley Wigger. (2019) *Invisible Companions: Encounters with Imaginary Friends, Gods, Ancestors, and Angels*. Stanford, CA: Stanford University Press.

Odo J. Zimmermann & Benedict R. Avery, trans. (nd) *Life and Miracles of St. Benedict: Book Two of the Dialogues by Pope Gregory the Great*. Collegeville, MN: Liturgical.

Additional Resources

Claudia Beeny. (2020) *What's Your Shine? A Method for Discovering Who You Are and Why It Matters*. Dallas: CKB Group.

Neil Douglas-Klotz. (1999) *The Hidden Gospel: Decoding the Spiritual Message of the Aramaic Jesus*. Wheaton, IL: Quest Books.

Elizabeth Hinson-Hasty. (2017) *The Problem of Wealth*. Maryknoll, NY: Orbis.

Elizabeth A. Johnson. (1992) *She Who Is: The Mystery of God in Feminist Theological Discourse*. New York: Crossroad.

Elizabeth A. Johnson. (2007) *Quest for the Living God: Mapping Frontiers in the Theology of God*. London. Continuum.

Lawrence Kushner. (2016) *God was in this Place & I, i did not know: Finding Self, Spirituality and Ultimate Meaning*. Woodstock, Vermont: Jewish Lights.

Amy-Jill Levine. (2006) *The Misunderstood Jew: The Church and the Scandal of the Jewish Jesus*. New York: HarperOne.

S. Painadath (2007) *We Are Co-Pilgrims: Towards a Culture of Inter-religious Harmony*. Delhi: Indian Society for Promoting Christian Knowledge.

S. Painadath. (2011) *The Power of Silence: Fifty Meditations to Discover the Divine Spirit Within You*. Delhi: Indian Society for Promoting Christian Knowledge.

Parker Palmer. (2000) *Let Your Life Speak: Listening for the Voice of Vocation*. San Francisco: Jossey Bass.

Eboo Patel. (2007) *Acts of Faith: The Story of an American Muslim, the Struggle for the Soul of a Generation.* Boston: Beacon.

Minna Proctor. (2005) *Do You Hear What I Hear? An Unreligious Writer Investigates Religious Calling.* New York: Penguin.

Alan Race. (1983) *Christians and Religious Pluralism: Patterns in the Christian Theology of Religions.* Maryknoll, NY: Orbis.

Richard Rohr. (2008) *Things Hidden: Scripture and Spirituality.* Cincinnati: St. Anthony Messenger.

Dominic White. (2015) *The Lost Knowledge of Christ: Contemporary Spiritualities, Christian Cosmology, and the Arts.* Collegeville, MN: Liturgical.

About the author

Melanie-Préjean Sullivan, DMin., is an educator and interspiritual chaplain in Louisville, Kentucky. Following careers in the museum field and secondary education, she retired from nearly twenty years in Catholic and interfaith university ministry. Currently, she teaches and facilitates conversations on the topics of spirituality, self-discovery, discernment, sacramental imagination, and on Church and Jewish history. She also serves as a visiting lecturer with the Margaret Beaufort Institute of Theology in Cambridge, England. Her book on teaching discernment, *Whispers, Nudges, and a Couple of Kicks* was recognized by the Catholic Campus Ministry Association for excellence in vocations ministry. She is a lay associate with the Sisters of the Eucharistic Covenant, is married, and has one son.

Made in the USA
Middletown, DE
16 April 2022

64038272R00076